Littl

Jesus, tl
Gentle

Best-selling parenting and children's book author, L.R.Knost, is an independent child development researcher and founder and director of the advocacy and consulting group, Little Hearts/Gentle Parenting Resources, as well as a monthly contributor to *The Natural Parent Magazine*. She is also a babywearing, breastfeeding, co-sleeping, homeschooling mother of six. Her children are a twenty-six-year-old married father of two; a twenty-four-year-old married Family Therapist working with at-risk children and families; a nineteen-year-old university pre-med student on scholarship; fifteen- and eight-year-old sweet, funny, socially active, homeschooled girls; and an adorable and active toddler. Other works by award-winning author, L.R.Knost, include *Two Thousand Kisses a Day: Gentle Parenting Through the Ages and Stages*, *Whispers Through Time: Communication Through the Ages and Stages of Childhood*, and *The Gentle Parent: Positive, Practical, Effective Discipline*, the first three books in the *Little Hearts Handbook* parenting guide series, as well as her children's picture books, *A Walk in the Clouds*, the soon-to-be-released *Grumpykins* series, and *Petey's Listening Ears*, the first in the *Wisdom for Little Hearts* series, which are humorous and engaging tools for parents, teachers, and caregivers to use in implementing gentle parenting techniques in their homes and schools.

*Note: Information contained in this book is for educational purposes only and should not be construed as medical or mental health counsel.

**Note: Several child-training manuals are referred to in this book for reference sake. These few were selected because of their name recognition and the popularity of their books, but they represent only a very small percentage of the pervasive spread of the child-training movement.

Jesus, the Gentle Parent
Gentle Christian Parenting

L.R.Knost

"Let your gentleness be evident to all."
Philippians 4:5

A Little Hearts Handbook
Little Hearts Books, LLC. ▪ U.S.A.

Photography credit: Melissa Lynsay Photography

Where did you learn love, child?
I felt it in my mommy's arms.

And where did you learn joy?
I heard it in my daddy's laugh.

Where did you learn peace, child?
I saw it in my mommy's life.

Where did you learn patience?
I heard it in my daddy's voice.

And where was kindness learned?
I felt it in my mommy's touch.

And what of goodness, child?
I saw it in my daddy's heart.

And where was faithfulness?
I heard it in my mommy's prayer.

And gentleness, my child?
I felt it in my daddy's hands.

And what of self-control?
I saw it in my mommy's eyes.

And what will you do with what you've learned?

I will love freely and share joy,
practice patience and self-control,
show kindness and pursue goodness,
and live a life of faithfulness
as I walk gently and in peace
through this wonderful world we share.

Love, joy, peace, patience, kindness, goodness,
faithfulness, gentleness, and self-control...

"And the greatest of these is love"

L.R.Knost

Table of Contents

Middle Childhood: Becoming Their Own Person

Gentle Parenting: Teens and Beyond

Appendix A

Appendix B

Appendix C

FOREWORD

Easter Sunday 2014
Jerusalem, Israel

Jesus, the Gentle Parent is a book to read, reread, and internalize.

In these pages, you will find keen insights and powerful Scriptural truths which I am only beginning to grasp the significance of, myself.

Before agreeing to write the foreword for *Jesus, The Gentle Parent*, I carefully read and examined how L.R. had engaged the subject, and I can say without hesitation that I am a better person, a better father, a better human being, and a better Christian for doing so.

I come from a background of high academic achievement in the area of Biblical studies. My late father, Dr. Ernest L. Martin (1932-2002), was one of the founding members of the Foundation for Biblical Research and an internationally recognized Biblical scholar with multiple books and academic credits to his name.

Growing up, I lived in Israel (my permanent adult residence since 2001) for five summers, living in the Bible lands while my father was involved in the largest excavation taking place in the Middle East at that time. For my summer vacations, I toured Biblical sites in Israel as well as visiting Greece and seeing where St. Paul journeyed.

I grew up in a house with a room dedicated to my father's library which numbered over 10,000 volumes when he passed away. These are the tools that I was taught to use. I've been exercising these tools now for some twenty years as I have studied and written exhaustively about doctrinal issues, including publishing a book on corporal punishment (spanking) in the Bible in the hope of shedding new light on that issue.

Echoing back some twenty-five years, another scholar who dramatically influenced me and provided what I call the spiritual anchors that allowed me to venture into new theological thinking was Dr. John Bradshaw, whose many books I highly recommend.

Dr. Bradshaw and I have a lot in common. We both have theological backgrounds, but the most important thing that I learned from Dr. Bradshaw is that people like me spend a lot of time in our heads.

We constantly think, analyze, try to figure out, solve, revise, review, research, and theorize on issues that are important to us. However, as

Dr. Bradshaw taught, and as I have come to see more and more as I approach the age of forty-nine as a married father of two girls, while spending time in your head is important, that time should not be spent at the expense of spending time in your heart. I won't bore you with an academic discussion on the "heart" in the Biblical context (as is my normal approach), but I will say this:

L.R. Knost's writing is some of the most powerful material you will ever read by anyone because it touches your heart.

L.R.'s books have absolute pure, transformative, healing power. I know. Every time I read anything L.R. writes, I feel the wonderful healing power in her words because L.R. writes with a view of healing your heart by connecting you to God's heart.

I read another of L.R.'s books, *Whispers Through Time*. What an amazing book of the heart it is. This book is pure heart, and it has helped me immensely to move out of my head and into my heart. It is so warm, quiet, peaceful, graceful, and tender, so motherly. It takes you by the hand and guides you back to your heart.

If I were to compare these two books from L.R. to a Biblical analogy, I am reminded that the prophet Elijah was known to have performed eight major miracles, while his successor, Elisha, was prophesied to have a double portion of the power of Elijah. Sure enough, Elisha performed sixteen major miracles. It is the same with L.R.Knost's new book, *Jesus, the Gentle Parent*, when compared to *Whisper's Through Time*.

Jesus, the Gentle Parent has a double portion of God's heart as L.R. brings her extensive experience as a mother and as a student of Scripture to share something with all of us that will make us use our hearts and our heads.

To be sure, this book has done exactly that for me. *Jesus, the Gentle Parent* has advanced my learning, head, heart, and everything else in between. It is my sincere prayer that the LORD will use this book to help make you and I more gentle parents as we move hour by hour towards the redemption that we have in Jesus Christ, our Lord. Amen.

Samuel S. Martin, Director of CenturyOne Foundation, Inc.
Project Coordinator of The New Foundation for Biblical Research
Author of *Thy Rod and Thy Staff, They Comfort Me: Christians and the Spanking Controversy*
Note: Samuel Martin's book can be downloaded free from -
http://whynottrainachild.com/2013/06/22/download-martins-book/

~ Introduction ~

Chapter 1

Jesus, the Gentle Parent

*"...a great and powerful wind tore the mountains apart and
shattered the rocks before the Lord, but the Lord was not in the
wind. After the wind there was an earthquake,
but the Lord was not in the earthquake.
After the earthquake came a fire,
but the Lord was not in the fire.
And after the fire came
a gentle whisper..."*
1 Kings 19:11-12

God has gone to great lengths, superhuman lengths even, to
reach out to his wandering children and call them home, back
into the safe shelter of his arms, into the warm welcome of his
presence, into the tender delight of his heart.

Throughout the Old Testament, he spoke through prophets,
dreams, angels, and even a bush! He revealed his character in his
'commandments' (in the original Hebrew text '*tsawah*' which
literally means '*directions*' or '*guides*')[1,2,3] and in the names he
called himself and in his interactions with that lovely, stubborn,
chosen nation, Israel.

And, finally, in the New Testament, he just stuck his feet right in
the dirt and somehow stuffed his infinite Being into the skin of a
human.

Jesus.

Emmanuel.

God with us.

GOD. *With.* Us!

Why in Heaven's name would he do that? Well, that's been the subject of dusty tomes and esoteric debates for centuries, but in truth the answer is very simple: God is a father, a daddy who wants to connect with and build a relationship with his children.

In the Old Testament God revealed himself as a father who is Creator, Provider, and Protector. He showed himself to be an involved father, interested in every detail of his children's lives, from what they ate to how and where and when they worshiped him. And he revealed his purity, his incomprehensible holiness that kept his beloved children hopelessly separated from him and helpless to change that fact. All the rules for cleansing, all the rituals, and all the formulas, only served to highlight the pitiful fallen state of God's beloved children.

Then, in the New Testament, God stepped in. He stepped out of Heaven, and he stepped into the muck and mire of life among his precious children.

And that ritualistic, external, temporal cleansing? It became relational, internal, and eternal.

Stones once thrown in righteous judgment were laid down in humble mercy. Punishment was replaced with grace as Righteousness Himself stood between sinful man and his dire fate.

And so we have Jesus, God Himself with us in the flesh, God's heart in a very literal sense laid bare for all the world to see, the perfect Parent to model ourselves after.

We have the Father...not a father, but THE Father...to look to for guidance about how to parent our children.

So, let's get practical. What does God's parenting look like, and how can we model ourselves after him?

Well, Jesus raised twelve children, so let's take a look at how he did it!

2

Twelve of God's children, all with different personalities, backgrounds, and talents, became Jesus' disciples. The word *disciple* is the root word in *discipline*, so in a completely literal sense to *discipline* our children means to *disciple* them.

So, what characteristics defined Jesus' discipleship? How did he treat his disciples? Was he harsh? Did he yell? Did he punish them? Clearly, he had the authority to! But since he came to free us from punishment, it really wouldn't make sense for him to start meting it out, would it?

Was he distant, unresponsive to their needs? Did he make demands, insist on instant obedience, and toss around kingly commands?

No, no, no, and no! Jesus treated his disciples gently, tenderly. He listened. He responded to their needs, answered their questions, spoke their language. Jesus encouraged and guided and taught his disciples.

He drew them close to himself, lived with them, ate with them, travelled with them. Jesus didn't just *say* he loved his disciples. He didn't simply *feel* love for his disciples. Jesus *lived* love for his disciples. And he lived that love daily, mercifully, sacrificially.

So, what are the characteristics that defined Jesus' discipleship?

Gentle. Tender. Responsive. Available.

Listening. Encouraging. Teaching. Guiding.

God, himself, intimately and empathetically connecting with his children.

That is perfect parenting.

I, however, am NOT a perfect parent. In the time it's taken me to write this so far, I've failed at pretty much every single one of those perfect parenting qualities. I only say that to point out that we aren't shooting for perfection here.

If perfection were possible, the Cross wouldn't have been necessary. (Galatians 2:21)

I have failed and will fail again as a parent. But even my failures have great value because they lead me back to the Cross, time and time again.

My failures remind me to turn to my perfect Parent, God, and trust him with my children. And my failures offer me the opportunity to be transparent with my children, to ask for forgiveness, to show them it's okay to be human and to make mistakes.

In short, my imperfections are perfect for demonstrating God's unconditional love.

So, what are some ways we can reflect Christ-like qualities in our never-perfect-but-best-effort parenting?

1. Build your relationship. Everything, absolutely everything, in raising children is dependent upon a secure parent/child relationship, and the foundation is trust. We talk all the time in Christian circles about needing to trust God more. Why? What's so important about trust? Trust is the secure knowledge that we will be cared for, that the person we are dependent on is who they say they are and will do what they say they will do. Without trust, there is no relationship. You build trust in your children starting from day one by responding faithfully and quickly to their needs, day or night, even if their 'need' is simply reassurance that you're there.

2. Be there in the moment. This isn't about quality time or quantity time. This is about actually being with your children when you're with them. I'm talking about muting the television and making sustained eye contact all the way through the story of how they had the piece of string first and how it was taken by a sibling when they only set it down for a minute and…well, you get the picture. Jesus showed he cared by listening and responding to what was important and relevant to his

children. Even when he was sound asleep on the boat, when his children cried out to him in fear, Jesus responded to their needs, soothed his children, and calmed the storm.

3. Encourage, don't discourage. Jesus built up his disciples, giving positive directions, allowing time and opportunity for them to try, helping when they needed it, and forgiving them when they failed. Never, not once, did he lash out at his disciples in anger. He taught them gently and encouragingly, often in stories that related to their daily lives, and he was always available to discuss or clarify or answer questions.

4. Practice what you preach. This is foundational, right along with trust. If you don't live out how you want your children to turn out, you can be pretty much guaranteed they'll go an entirely different way. Listen to your children if you want them to learn to listen. Respect your children if you want them to learn respect. Model compassion, kindness, honesty, forgiveness, and a grateful spirit if you want your children to grow into adults with those character traits. Jesus certainly lived out every one of those qualities for his children.

5. Don't make excuses. If you fail (and you will) *apologize*. Nothing penetrates hurt more deeply and with more healing power than an honest, open apology.

6. Give grace. The unconditional love of God is beyond human comprehension. Even 'veteran' Christians resort to trying to earn God's grace when they've already been given it freely. We all fall into that trap, time and time again, because we just can't wrap our human brains around something as awesomely simple as unconditional love. We think it MUST be more complicated, and we end up complicating it by trying to pay for something that is free! So, help your children while they're looking to you, their earthly parent, for an example of how their Heavenly Parent operates. Give them grace. Guide them gently. Forgive them when

they fall, and get down on their level to help them back up again.

7. Enjoy your blessings. Your children are a reward, a blessing, a gift straight from the heart of your Father to you, his precious child. He wants you to feel what he feels, to experience him in a unique way through parenting your children in the way that he parents you. He wants you to delight in your children so you'll understand how he delights in you. He wants you to feel the depth of concern he feels when you stray into danger, the heights of joy he feels when you run trustingly into his arms, the pangs of compassion he feels when you are hurting or scared. Take the time to enjoy your children, and you will find yourself closer to the heart of your Father than you can possibly imagine.

"Whoever receives one of these little children in My name receives Me; and whoever receives Me, receives not Me but Him who sent Me."
Mark 9:37

~ A Gentle Beginning ~

Chapter 2

Tattered Tapestries:
Weaving Trust through the Chaos

"For I know the plans I have for you," declares
the Lord, "plans to prosper you and not to harm you,
plans to give you hope and a future."
Jeremiah 29:11

.....

The old preacher's slightly shaky voice and once-hearty arthritic
hands spoke of life and experience and hard-won wisdom as he
held up a dusty tapestry with the back facing us. The tangle of
threads that seemed to go nowhere and the snarl of multicolored
knots gave no hint of the picture on the other side. "This is what
we see," he said. Then he turned the tapestry around to display
the intricate, painstakingly crafted, exquisite picture on the front
side. "And this is what God is doing." He looked around the
room, a kind and gentle understanding in his age-dimmed gaze.
"Faith is trusting that your Father's hands are carefully
weaving a beautiful life's story, even when all you can see is
chaos."

I remember this story often when life feels overwhelming, when
big things like layoffs and sicknesses hit, and when small things
like cranky toddlers, piles of laundry, and broken refrigerators
annoy. What feels to me like an endless cycle of dishes and
diapers, punctuated by the odd disaster, must look like brilliant
threads of golden perseverance, scarlet sacrifice, and soft blue-
grey shades of faith, all woven tenderly into my life's tapestry
by my Father's skillful hands.

I imagine life feels this way to my children, as well. They may not see the picture I am trying to weave as I teach and guide and nourish and encourage them to grow into the beautiful humans they were created to be.

They may not understand why they're gently redirected when they try to crawl up the stairs or why bugs don't make a good afternoon snack. They may not be able to fathom why their new dragonfly 'pet' can't live in the house or why they can't hide in "the best hiding place EVER" in a hot car on a steamy Florida afternoon. They may not be entirely thrilled with the agreement on no laptops in their rooms or no cell phone in their tween years, and they may not fully get why the mall is not a safe hangout spot and why periodic texts to check in when out with friends are part of our family dynamic in their teen years.

As my children grow old enough to participate in the decision making, though, we share our thoughts about these things, discuss them together, and come up with mutually agreed upon boundaries. While these things may seem like meaningless threads or even unnecessary knots and tangles in their lives, the trust that we share helps them to accept and cooperate with what they may not fully understand, knowing that I have a purpose for each of these things even if they can't see it.

It is that trust, that faith in my motives, my wisdom, my love, that makes gentle parenting possible. I don't have to 'lay down the law' or enforce 'rules' with punishments or 'control' my children with threats or intimidation because they know that I have their best interests at heart and that I will always, always listen to their concerns, even if I can't change things or give them what they want.

I start building that trust from the moment my children are born and continue building it throughout their childhood. I respond quickly, consistently, and with empathy to their cries or whines or troubles whether they are eight days, eight years, or eighteen years old. I meet their needs as fully as I am able, whether those needs are a clean diaper, a full belly, a listening ear, or a warm hug. I try to always respond gently and thoughtfully to their behaviors, whether they are having a meltdown, whining, tattling, questioning, or even challenging me.

And, perhaps most importantly, I'm honest about my own imperfections. I'm willing to apologize when I make one of my many human parenting mistakes, and I don't expect perfection from my equally human children.

Motherhood is very simple to me. It's a gift *to* me, but it's not *about* me. I'm the one who chose to bring these little people into the world, so the pervading belief in our modern culture that somehow they have the responsibility to fit into *my* life, and work around *my* schedule, and not disrupt *my* pursuits completely mystifies me. They aren't interlopers; they are guests, *invited* guests. And how do we treat our guests? Do we ignore their needs or make incomprehensible demands on them or ridicule, name-call, and hit them when they misstep? Of course not. We welcome our guests with special dinners, make accommodations for their needs, and forgive their lack of knowledge of our ways. And our children deserve no less. In fact, they deserve much more.

In our home, when our newest little invited guests arrive, they are welcomed with open arms that are always available, day or night. They are provided nature's best provision for their nutritional needs. And they are gently guided by example and lovingly encouraged to become a part of a healthy family dynamic. In short, when I invite these little people into my life, it stops being *my* life, and it becomes *our* lives.

Parenthood is, very simply, a beautiful sacrifice that mothers and fathers willingly and lovingly live for their children, day after day, night after night, as a reflection of the sacrifice Jesus made for his children on the Cross. Parenthood is a lovely, lively retelling of the Cross played out in the arms of mamas and daddies, again and again and again.

Consider the young mother who gives up night after night of sleep to soothe her little one's cries, or the middle aged man who still gets up before dawn each day to provide for his family, or the elderly parents who give up the peace of their golden years to welcome the child of their youth back into their home when life hits hard. This laying down of self, this giving up of comforts and rights and dreams, these are losses, sacrifices, even hardships, but they are lovely, beautiful beyond belief. Their loveliness lies in the soft warmth of a sleepy baby with a full belly and a trusting heart. Their beauty lies in the joyful chaos of a messy, noisy, welcoming family to come home to each night. Their beauty lies in the spark of hope in the tear-filled eyes of a weary adult whose life has turned dark, but who finds that home is still a safe refuge.

My children, all six of them, are precious gifts straight from God's heart to my home. I have had other precious gifts, babies whom God gave for a time to fill my womb, but who weren't meant to fill my arms, and one He gave to fill my arms for a just a moment in time, but who wasn't meant to stay. My stillborn son, Sammy's, birthday is in just a few weeks. While he's always in my heart, as his birthday approaches my heart tightens in my chest a bit more each day until the ache becomes almost unbearable, and then finally the day comes and goes and I can breathe again.

These times always make me wonder how tragedy must look from Heaven's side. I wonder about my Sammy, and I wonder about my other lost babies, gone before they even had birthdays. What colors did they add to my story? What eternal beauty did they bring that would have made my tapestry incomplete if they had not come and gone, so heartbreakingly briefly, into my life? While I feel holes in my heart, one for each much-wanted child, and an aching cavern of loss for my Sammy, would my life have been complete without them?

I can't answer these questions. I won't even try. But I imagine that is where faith stretches its silken blue-grey threads across my story like the fragile gossamer wings of a butterfly. Each one of them brought with them the unique knowledge of how breathtakingly exquisite every living, breathing child is and how priceless and fragile and brief life itself can be. I do not take this knowledge lightly. I have learned to treasure the moments of life with my children. I've learned that it's not about me; it's about us. And I've learned that sacrifice lights up the dark places in the world, making it a more beautiful place for all of us to live.

Life is messy. No one has all the answers, at least not earth-side. But we can all trust that this sometimes bewildering, sometimes joyful, sometimes flat-out painful chaos called life has meaning and purpose and beauty beyond the scope of human sight. And as we carefully and gently weave the strands of our children's days into a beautiful childhood, we can trust that our Father is thoughtfully and tenderly doing the same for us.

"Now we see through a glass darkly; then we shall see clearly, face to face. Now I know in part, then I shall know fully, even as I am fully known."
1 Corinthians 13:12

Chapter 3

Hand-Crafted by God: Handle with Care

"Before I created you in the womb I knew you;
before you were born I set you apart"
Jeremiah 1:5

A tiny child cries in the night. In one family a parent responds with comfort, meeting needs and soothing cries, while another family reacts with correction, often by ignoring the cries. In each case, the child is deeply loved, so what causes the different responses?

The parents' perception of sin.

The first family sees a child expressing a human need in the God-given way that all healthy babies communicate. The second family sees a child manifesting a heart of sin, self-centered and selfish, manipulating to get its needs met.

The fundamental difference in these parents' understanding of the concept of a 'sin nature' produces a profound difference in their parental choices and responses and, by extension, in the messages their parenting sends to their children. The first parents are focused on building a relationship by meeting needs, offering comfort, and creating trust. The second parents are focused on correcting an in-built flaw and establishing their authority, often because they are acting on ideas such as the following, taught by fundamentalists in their child-training manuals:

"Even a child in the womb and coming from the womb is wayward and sinful" (pg. 12)...The child is a sinner. There are things within the heart of the sweetest little baby that, allowed to blossom and grow to fruition, will bring about eventual destruction. The rod functions in this context" (p. 105).[4]
(Tedd Tripp, Shepherding a Child's Heart)

"...this tendency toward self-will is the essence of 'original sin'
which has infiltrated the human family. It certainly explains why

I place such stress on the proper response to willful defiance during childhood, for that rebellion can plant the seeds of personal disaster."⁵ (Dr. James Dobson, Dare to Discipline)

"When should a parent start using the rod of correction on a child that the Lord has brought into the family? ... A child very quickly demonstrates his fallen, depraved nature and reveals himself to be a selfish little beast in manifold ways. As soon as the child begins to express his own self-will (and this occurs early in life) that child needs to receive correction. My wife and I have a general goal of making sure that each of our children has his will broken by the time he reaches the age of one year. To do this, a child must receive correction when he is a small infant."⁶ (Ronald E. Williams, The Correction and Salvation of Children)

But here's the thing, babies aren't born with an in-built flaw. They are born perfect. God handcrafts every human. He said so himself. His work is perfect. He said so himself. Little humans are made in God's image, formed by the very hands that created the universe, and spoken into life by the very voice that called everything he created, "Good." (Genesis 1:31)

Jesus, himself, is not only fully God, he was also fully human, formed in the womb, known by his Father before his birth, and filled with life by the breath of God.

Jesus.

Fully human.

Fully perfect.

No in-built flaw from the hands of God.

Believing that babies are formed by God in the womb with a fatal flaw and are therefore born as sinners, liars, and manipulators simply doesn't make sense. It doesn't add up in light of God's perfection, his love, his wisdom.

Father. Son. Holy Spirit.

Perfection. Love. Wisdom.

These three combine to create God's children, his perfect children, in his image, his perfect image.

So what, then, is the 'sin nature' that is spoken of in God's Word? Sin nature, in and of itself, is not sin. It is, instead, the *capability* to sin. It is only in our *choices* when we are old enough to be *conscious* of sin, in how we use God's gift of free will, that sin enters the picture. And it is on the Cross, not in an establishment of authority, not in a demand for obedience, not in a display of power, but in the love of a gentle Savior, that sin exits the picture.

That is where grace was born…on an old rugged Cross, in a heart overflowing with unconditional love, in eyes that saw God's precious children lost and in need, in a voice that cried out, *"It is finished!" (John 19:30)* in a death, a burial, and a resurrection. And that grace, so painfully and sacrificially won for us, is what we can…no, is what we *must* share with our children.

We are our children's first experience of God. How we treat them, how we respond to them, what we model for them, those are all images of parenthood that are imprinted on our children's hearts from the moment of birth, and they will carry those images with them for life. God's unconditional love, his gentleness, his compassion, his acceptance, his sacrifice…those are the images our children need to see reflected in our parenting, to have tenderly woven into the fabric of their childhood, to carry forever as whispered memories etched on their hearts, echoing the heart of God.

"Follow God's example, therefore, as dearly loved children and walk in the way of love, just as Christ loved us and gave himself up for us as a fragrant offering and sacrifice to God."
Ephesians 5:1-2

Chapter 4

Breastfeeding: Manna from God

> *"But we proved to be gentle among you,*
> *as a nursing mother tenderly cares for her own children."*
> *1 Thessalonians 2:7*

Jesus' mother, Mary, didn't practice attachment parenting when raising little Jesus. The Bible does tell us that she breastfed Jesus, *"Blessed is the mother who gave you birth and nursed you." (Luke 11:27).* The culture of the time tells us that she likely coslept with him in the small, one or two room house typical of that period and that she wore him close to her heart in the daylight hours in a wrap to keep him safe from the snakes and scorpions and other dangers that populated the region. So it is certain that she was a breastfeeding mama and almost certain that she was a cosleeping and babywearing mama.

But Mary didn't practice attachment parenting as she was growing a tiny Savior. She simply parented Jesus in the naturally instinctive way that mothers have mothered their little ones since time began. Attachment parenting is merely a term coined much later to tie these natural parenting choices and others in with the modern research of psychologists like John Bowlby who found that the healthiest emotional and relational adults tended to have strong early attachments with a parent or primary caregiver.

The Bible reinforces those research findings by not just referring to breastfeeding as providing life-sustaining nutrition, but also as a source of comfort and connection, *"For you will nurse and be satisfied at her comforting breasts." (Isaiah 66:11)*

God's biological design for breastfeeding weaves a developing infant's needs with a mother's needs into a delicately synchronized dance, and even daddies get in on the dance! There is an inbuilt, biochemical response to the birth of a baby that affects both sexes in similar, though somewhat different ways. As the birth of a new baby nears, a mother's oxytocin level, known as the 'love hormone' because of its ability to create warm feelings of safety and attachment, increases as part of the preparation for bringing a new life into the world and sustaining that life at her breast. Daddies also experience a rise in oxytocin, as well as an increase in estrogen, which results in their brains being pre-wired to love and protect their mate and offspring. Then, after birth and throughout the breastfeeding relationship, oxytocin levels in mamas and daddies remain elevated, rising and falling in rhythmic peaks and valleys in response to a baby's ever-changing needs.[7] This is no accident of nature. This is a beautiful biological design.

This lovely and perfect design also reveals itself in the balance of nutrients present in breastmilk. Breastmilk has the perfect composition of calories, nutrients, fats, and other components to ensure the optimal development of a growing infant. The composition of breastmilk shifts to accommodate growth spurts, sicknesses, and other needs throughout a mother and child's nursing relationship. Interestingly, the ratios of each of the components change throughout the day to offer the most energy during the daylight hours and the highest concentrations of sleep-inducing nucleotides during nighttime feeding, so if a mama is pumping and storing breastmilk, it's important to label the time of day the milk was pumped to avoid giving the more stimulating daytime milk at night![8]

Beyond the nutritional and bonding benefits of breastfeeding, there are also amazing health benefits to both mama and baby:

> A reduction in the risk of SIDS, asthma, childhood leukemia, diabetes, gastroenteritis, otitis media (ear infections), LRTIs (pneumonia, bronchitis, etc), necrotizing enterocolitis, and obesity are just some of the protective benefits for babies. For mothers, breastfeeding has been correlated with a significant decrease in the risk of diseases such as breast cancer, ovarian cancer, diabetes, and heart disease to name just a few.[9]

Additionally, the Journal of the American Academy of Pediatrics released a study in April of 2010 that concluded, "The United States incurs $13 billion in excess costs annually and suffers 911 preventable deaths per year because our breastfeeding rates fall far below medical recommendations."[9] Those numbers are only based on breastfeeding benefits for the first six months of life. The World Health Organization, American Academy of Pediatrics, Centers for Disease Control, and others recommend breastfeeding for the first two years of a child's life. Imagine the tally if the researchers had looked at the lives lost and billions of dollars spent unnecessarily in a two year breastfeeding scenario instead of a six month scenario. (*Two Thousand Kisses a Day: Gentle Parenting Through the Ages and Stages*)

Some stumbling blocks in the breastfeeding relationship that mamas may encounter include the modern societal view of breasts as solely sexual objects which often leads those in public places, including many churches, to shame mothers into hiding in restrooms or vehicles or at the very least using covers that make breastfeeding far more difficult and clumsy than it needs to be. Biblically speaking, breasts are referred to half as often in reference to sexual relationships as they are in reference to the God-designed breastfeeding relationship between mothers and their little ones. Again, that is no accident!

Breastfeeding is not shameful and should not be hidden. As one of our current world leaders, Pope Francis, said during a 2014 baptism ceremony at the historic Sistine Chapel,

> *"Today the choir will sing, but the most beautiful choir of all is the choir of the infants who will make a noise. Some will cry because they are not comfortable or because they are hungry," Francis said, according to Reuters. "If they are hungry, mothers, feed them, without thinking twice. Because they are the most important people here."[10]*

He didn't tell them to leave or to cover up or to make their babies wait. He tenderly told the young mothers to feed their babies when they're hungry. End of story.

Another stumbling block to a healthy, full-term breastfeeding relationship is the increasingly prevalent diagnosis of low milk supply:

> Even though mothers' bodies are capable of miraculously growing a human being for nine months and bringing that precious new life into the world, those same life-giving bodies seem to be failing in ever-increasing numbers to provide life-giving nutrition to those precious babies because of issues with low milk supply.

> Why is this happening? For some, it is certainly just pediatricians using formula-fed babies' growth charts instead of breastfed babies' charts or family and friends who believe that all babies should be chubby and content that lead new mothers to believe they have low supply, but there does appear to be an increasing number of babies legitimately labeled as failure-to-thrive with low milk supply determined to be the cause.[9] (*Two Thousand Kisses a Day: Gentle Parenting Through the Ages and Stages*)

Often the low milk supply is caused by forcing babies to sleep alone and training them to sleep through the night. The fact is that babies aren't biologically designed to sleep through the night. They are, though, biologically programmed to crave closeness with their mothers, and their proximity to and access to the breast throughout the night stimulates ongoing production of breastmilk, keeping up the mother's supply naturally.[11] As a simple matter of survival, it makes biological sense that God would build into babies a need to be near their primary source of safety, nutrition, and comfort:

> Babies biologically should not sleep through the night. Not only is the deep sleep required to sleep through the night actually a recognized factor in SIDS (Sudden Infant Death Syndrome),[12] but babies who sleep

through the night are also not nursing to stimulate breastmilk production, thus their mother's milk may begin to dry up. Clearly, that's not a healthy biological design. (*Two Thousand Kisses a Day: Gentle Parenting Through the Ages and Stages*)

The bottom line is that breastfeeding is a biological norm created by God to meet a baby's needs in the healthiest and most convenient way. That said, there are certainly times when a mother can't breastfeed due to a medical condition, life circumstances, adoption, or other factors. In those cases mamas can still achieve a healthy attachment and strong, loving relationship and even boost their oxytocin 'love hormone' levels[13] by holding their little ones close to their hearts during feeding, making eye contact and exchanging smiles and coos and giggles, kissing and nuzzling their babies' fuzzy little heads, keeping their little ones close during the day in a baby wrap or sling, taking time out for a few periods of 'kangaroo care'[14] each day, and meeting nighttime needs quickly, gently, and consistently.

"For I was hungry and you gave me something to eat, I was thirsty and you gave me something to drink, I was a stranger and you invited me in, I needed clothes and you clothed me, I was sick and you looked after me..."
Matthew 25:35-40

Chapter 5

Cosleeping: The ~~Marriage~~ Family Bed

"You shall call, and the Lord will answer;
You shall cry, and he will say, 'Here I am.'"
Isaiah 58:9

The darkness of the night can be a fearsome and lonely time even for adults, so the idea that babies and small children need to be left to face the darkness alone so they can learn to self-soothe is incomprehensible to me. Nighttime needs are no less important than daytime needs. In fact, in many ways nighttime needs are actually more important than daytime needs not only because of heightened fears, but for the simple reason that the deep of the night is when the busyness of the day stills, hearts are more open, and voices are softer, creating the opportunity to really connect and communicate on the deepest heart level.

It is in those moments in the quiet stillness that my teens and tweens talk about life and death and dreams and challenges and triumphs and failures. We work through problems together, process those big adolescent and preadolescent emotions, and cement our trust relationship. And all of that has its roots in those first days and weeks and months when I laid the foundation for that trust relationship, night after night, gentle response after gentle response.

In many Christian circles, child-training is taught as the key to good parenting, and sleep training is where parents are told that it should begin. In Chapter Ten, we'll talk about the interesting translations of the "train up a child" verse in the Bible and how it fits into gentle Christian parenting, but for now let's focus on the issue of sleep training.

The thing is, humans don't learn to soothe themselves by being left to soothe themselves. We were designed by a relational God to be relational beings and, therefore, to learn and grow and have our needs met through our relationships, both with him, our heavenly Father, and with our earthly parents and then, over time, with other family members and friends. In God's perfect design, peace and contentment are shared from parent to child, not through ignoring needs, but through meeting needs. Our little ones don't need to be trained to soothe themselves to sleep; they need to be parented to sleep by our soothing presence, comfort, and support.

Even adults, the most emotionally healthy ones anyway, don't self-soothe when they are in distress. Just the opposite, they reach out to trusted family and friends for comfort and support, whereas emotionally unhealthy adults often try to self-soothe by things like reaching for a beer or a cigarette or overeating for comfort, or, worse, drowning their needs in alcoholism or escaping their needs with illicit drugs or engaging in damaging relationships to try to get their needs met.

In the same way that it is *starving* children who crave food, not children whose hunger needs are met, it is the adults whose comfort and attachments needs were *not* met in childhood who cannot satisfy their cravings as adults no matter what they try to fill them with, not adults whose childhood needs were fully, gently, and consistently met.

God says of himself, *"When they cry out to me, I will hear, for I am compassionate," (Exodus 22:27b)* and, *"I am he who comforts you," (Isaiah 51:12)* and in the New Testament we read, *"Praise be to...the Father of compassion and the God of all comfort, who comforts us in all our troubles, so that we can comfort those in any trouble with the comfort we ourselves receive from God." (2 Corinthians 1:3-4)*

In contrast to how God describes his own responsive parenting to us, though, some of the well-known names in the world of child-training insist that parents must resist their God-given parental instincts and ignore their children's cries:

> *"Mothering decisions without assessment are dangerous. Such noncognitive responses violate the*

Bible's call to sober-mindedness (Ezzo, Prep for Parenting p.142)[15]...she simply reacts to her feelings when she hears her baby cry. Yet feelings never were and never will be the basis for any sound decision-making ...Why would intuition suddenly assume center stage in this, her most critical role? (Ezzo, Babywise, p.150)[16]...Women who demand feed say they love their children because they tend to their every need. That is not Biblical love; it's idolatry."[15] (Gary Ezzo, Prep for Parenting, p.142)

"The pitiful look of betrayal in his poor little eyes just breaks her suffering heart. It would hurt her too much to obey God in training up her child ... To set aside one's own feelings for the purpose of objectivity regarding the good of the child is the only true love."[17] (Michael Pearl, To Train Up a Child).

How though, with God himself as our guide, can we deny our children comfort and compassion when they are lonely, uncomfortable, and scared? And, to return to the truth of a perfect design by a perfect Father, the fact is that babies are biologically programmed to wake frequently at night as a matter of survival.[12] As we discussed in the last chapter, breastfeeding success or failure is often tied in to how much proximity and access to the breast babies have throughout the night to keep their milk supply stimulated, so in ages past, before formula was invented, babies very lives depended on night-wakings to keep the breastfeeding mothers' milk from drying up. Other considerations also play into this perfect biological design:

Small children tend to differ not in whether they wake at night or not, but in whether they need help in being soothed back to sleep or not based on their own unique personalities, health issues, environmental factors, etc. Sleeping patterns are neither a sign of a 'good' baby or a 'bad' baby, just a normal baby. In fact, even adults tend to wake frequently at night, but typically just roll over or adjust their blankets or take a quick trip to the bathroom and then go back to sleep. They just don't often remember any of it in the morning!

In reality, night-waking is simply a biological norm[12] that has been misconstrued as 'problems sleeping' or 'sleep issues' by the demands of our modern, hectic lifestyle. All of those factors, together with the benefit of round-the-clock stimulation of breastmilk production in those first all-important months, makes responding to your baby's nighttime needs as normal and necessary as responding to their daytime needs. (*Two Thousand Kisses a Day: Gentle Parenting Through the Ages and Stages*)

Of course, a need for reassurance and comfort is as worthy of a response as a need for sustenance, and responding to our little one's needs swiftly and consistently is the foundation of gentle parenting as we build that early trust relationship that will be the bedrock upon which we base our connection, communication, and discipline in the years to come. Cosleeping is just an umbrella term that covers several ways of simplifying the meeting of nighttime needs:

Cosleeping is simply the age-old mother's way of meeting a baby's nighttime needs in the most convenient and natural way possible. Cosleeping can consist of room-sharing, using a side-car attached to your bed, or actually bed-sharing. Room-sharing and using a side-car attachment are no different when it comes to safety measures than putting your baby in their own room as long as you follow the normal safety standards of avoiding crib bumpers and loose sheets, pillows, stuffed animals, blankets, etc. The advantages of room-sharing or using a side-car attachment are, of course, speed and ease in responding to your little one's nighttime needs as well as providing them with the comfort of your presence nearby.

Bed-sharing is the cosleeping option in which your baby sleeps in bed with you. Many new mamas admit to accidentally falling asleep while nursing their little ones, but that can be dangerous if bed-sharing safety recommendations aren't followed. Those recommendations include the same care in avoiding loose sheets, pillows, stuffed animals, and blankets along with making sure that no one other than a healthy, non-drinking, non-smoking, non-drug using parent is the only one allowed to bed-share with your baby. Before considering co-sleeping, be sure to read all of the safety recommendations from Dr. James J. McKenna, Ph.D. Professor of Biological Anthropology, Director, Mother-Baby Sleep Laboratory, University of Notre Dame.[18]

The advantages of bed-sharing, in addition to the aforementioned speed and ease of response to nighttime needs and the comfort of your presence, are in the increased stimulation of breastmilk production similar to that of kangaroo-care (skin-to-skin) and, as studies have shown, the matching of circadian rhythms (wake/sleep cycles) in mothers and infants which may allow mothers to feel more rested despite the interrupted sleep inherent in caring for a young baby.[11]
(Two Thousand Kisses a Day: Gentle Parenting Through the Ages and Stages)

Whatever the sleeping arrangements, though, the real key is simply being able to meet nighttime needs quickly and safely. Meeting nighttime needs does involve a lot of sacrifice, and it can feel like we'll never get caught up on our sleep again, but the high-needs season of a baby's life is far more brief than it feels in those exhausting watches of the night, and the trust relationship we are building will be well worth the sacrifice in the years to come.

"Do not fear, for I am with you; do not be afraid, for I am your God. I will strengthen you; I will help you; I will hold on to you with my righteous right hand."
Isaiah 41:10

Chapter 6

Babywearing: Heartbeat to Heartbeat

"He tends his flock like a shepherd
He gathers the lambs in his arms and
carries them close to his heart."
Isaiah 40:11

....

Laundry sorted, dishes done
Snuggling my little one
Hands free to do my daily tasks
Even when "Hold you?" she asks
Off we go now to the store
Where naptime comes with gentle snore
As tucked against my heart she sleeps
Then, shopping done, I kiss soft cheeks
While waking eyes blink up at me
A smile curves contentedly
Across her tiny little face
She's woken in her favorite place
Then down to toddle off she goes
'Til small legs tire and she slows
Then back to babywearing we
Will go, my little one and me

A fascinating study in Israel in 2011 found that a simple, loving smile between a mother and her child can synchronize their hearts, causing them to beat in harmony, heartbeat to heartbeat.[19] What a lovely way to connect, gazing into our little ones' eyes, hearts beating in tune as we smile at one another, isn't it?

The Three C's of gentle parenting are Connection, Communication, and Cooperation, with connection being the starting point. Building that connection through babywearing in the first weeks and months and years, keeping our little ones close enough for kisses and smiles and cuddles throughout the day, is not only convenient, it's also a beautiful picture of how God carries us close to his heart and a lovely way of conveying the image of an always close, always available, always loving heavenly Father.

And, really, what could possibly be more wonderful than simply tipping your head to kiss a little nose, nuzzle a fuzzy little head, and look into the owl-eyed gaze of your sweet newborn? How precious to exchange giggles and grins with your adorable baby and share the world with your curious toddler while sharing an eye-to-eye and heart-to-heart view of the world?

Beyond even these wonders of babywearing and the convenience of offering hands-free time for busy parents, babywearing also has some very valuable and practical advantages for our little ones including replacing tummy-time for babies who don't enjoy being stuck on the floor. While upright in a baby wrap or structured carrier, a baby's core and neck muscles are being strengthened by the motion of a parent's body as they walk and bend and move throughout the day.[20] And the benefits don't stop there:

> The incidence of plagiocephaly, or flat-head syndrome, has increased dramatically[21] since the medical community began recommending infants sleep on their backs to reduce the risk of SIDS. While babies should certainly sleep on their backs, they don't need to spend their days in carriers, strollers, bouncers, and swings, or lying flat on their backs on playmats or blankets, which only increase the amount of pressure to a baby's still-flexible skull bones, resulting in a flattened area that may require a helmet to remold it into a normal shape. Babywearing reduces the amount of time infants spend on their backs, thus reducing or even eliminating the risk of plagiocephaly.
>
> Since most babies naturally desire to be close to their source of food and comfort, babies tend to be calmer and more content when being worn[14] than when they

are left alone, though there is always that unique baby who likes his or her own space. Babywearing, as with all other options for parenting gently, needs to be adapted to suit a little one's own personality and needs. Some high-needs babies may do better taking naps during the day while being worn, giving mama a hands-free break while still meeting her baby's needs. Other babies do well being worn after nursing to aid in digestion, reducing gassiness and the incidence of reflux.[22]

Babywearing also aids in hip health when using a properly designed carrier. *The International Hip Dysplasia Institute* has warned against excessive amounts of time in car seats, walkers, swings, and other devices that keep babies' legs extended and pushed together. Their recommendation is for a baby's legs to be in the 'frog' position, with their thighs supported and their knees bent.[23] This is the positioning you should look for when shopping for a carrier to wear your little one. (*Two Thousand Kisses a Day: Gentle Parenting Through the Ages and Stages*)

Wearing your baby against your heart, where the slightest tilt of your head brings your smile into focus for your tiny one, is not only one of the most beautiful and bonding experiences you can have with your little one, but clearly also has benefits far beyond our understanding. The options for babywearing are extensive and can be a bit overwhelming, so be sure to look for a lending library or 'Sling Meet' in your area to try out the styles available to find the one that will work best for you and also check out www.littleheartsbooks.com for links to product reviews and recommendations.

"As one whom his mother comforts, So I will comfort you"
Isaiah 66:11

Chapter 7

A Sea Change: Obedience is Not the Goal

*"Look also at ships: although they are so large and are driven
by fierce winds, they are turned by a very small rudder
wherever the pilot desires."
James 3:4*

Oh, the toddler years, those delightful days when little ones
begin to discover that they are, indeed, separate individuals from
their parents and begin to test the waters to see how far out to
sea their little boats can take them when they've got a full head
of steam. This is the age when parents begin to wonder how in
the world to tether their little steamboats to the docks or scuttle
them in shallow waters to slow them down.

Obedience becomes a hot topic at moms' groups and men's
breakfasts, at playdates and on park benches as parents wrestle
with this new developmental stage that often shows up,
unwelcome and unannounced, and the desperate, bewildered
question being debated is always the same:

"How can I get my child to obey?"

Take a moment and examine what that question really means,
though. Does it mean, *"How can I control my child?"* or does it
mean, *"How can I help my child learn self-control?"* It's an
important distinction because the first meaning is external and
temporary (i.e. only effective as long as the controlling factors
are ever-present and escalate as the child grows) and the second
meaning is internal and intrinsic. In the first, the rudder of a
child's ship is firmly removed from the child's hands again and

again as the parent and child struggle for control of the ship. In the second, the rudder remains in the child's hands as the parent guides, instructs, and leads the way with their little steamboat sheltered alee of the parent ship.

Parents often feel lost at sea, themselves, when it comes to the best course for guiding and growing their children in the storm-tossed waves and murky waters of childhood behaviors, and many churches try to meet parent's needs by offering parenting books and classes. A vast number of those resources are, unfortunately, based on a punitive, authoritarian model. These books, and the classes based on the books, claim to be Biblical, but miss the heart of the Father entirely and mislead and even intimidate parents into believing that they must train their children into instant, unquestioning obedience in order to raise their children 'God's way.'

Consider, though, that Jesus said, *"You will know them by their fruit." (Matthew 7:16)* referring to how we will recognize his children. And what is the fruit of the Spirit? Love. Joy. Peace. Patience. Kindness. Goodness. Gentleness. Faithfulness. Self-control. What's missing? Nothing. God's Word is perfect. And yet obedience is not included as a fruit of the Spirit. It is not mentioned as a measure of love for God or evidence of a relationship with God. That certainly doesn't mean that God doesn't want us to listen to his wise counsel and remain within the safe boundaries he's shared with us. What it does mean is that it's a heart issue, not an obedience issue, and he wants our trust and thoughtful, considered cooperation, not our fear-driven, mindless obedience.

Did you know, in fact, that the word *obey* doesn't even appear in the original texts of the Bible? When the English translators of the King James version of the Bible encountered the Hebrew words *hupakouo/hupakoe* and *shema/lishmoa* they discovered that there wasn't an exact English equivalent, so they chose the word *hearken* in their translations which subsequently became an archaic term and was later changed to *obey*.[24] So, what exactly do the original words in the Bible mean?

Hupakouo/hupakoe – to hear from above; to listen for; to lend an ear to[1,2,3]

Shama/lishmoa – to understand, to internalize, to ponder, to reflect upon[1,2,3]

And, in the negative form, rather than the word *disobedience* in the original texts, there is…

Parakouo – to close one's ears to; to ignore[1,2,3]

The same mistranslation also occurs from the original Greek texts of the New Testament where *peitho* and *peitharcheo* are translated into, respectively, *obey* and *disobey* but actually mean…

Peitho – to be persuaded; to be moved; to respond[25]

Peitharcheo – to remain unpersuaded; to be unmoved by; to be unresponsive to[25]

Taken together, the meaning of what is now translated *obey* in the original text of the Bible is more accurately read *'listen to, thoughtfully consider, and respond to.'* That is a far, far different meaning than the 'instant obedience' often held up as the epitome of Christian faith and evidence of love for God and, by extension, the goal of so-called 'Biblical parenting.'

Before we address the parenting conundrum of instant obedience versus thoughtful consideration, let's look at several verses in the Bible with the original meanings restored:

He replied, "Blessed rather are those who hear the Word of God and ~~obey~~ listen to, thoughtfully consider, and respond to it." (Luke 11:28)

Jesus replied, "Anyone who loves me will ~~obey~~ listen to, thoughtfully consider, and respond to my teaching. My Father will love them, and we will come to them and make our home with them. (John 14:23)

Children, ~~obey~~ listen to, thoughtfully consider, and respond to your parents in the Lord, for this is right. (Ephesians 6:1)

One other interesting note is that the word translated *punish* in the English versions of the Bible is from the Hebrew word *avon* and from the Greek *kolasis/kolazo*. Look at the contrast in meanings:

Punish (English) - to inflict a penalty upon; to exact retribution; to make suffer[26]

Avon (Hebrew) – to carry guilt; to bear one's own iniquity[1,2,3]

Kolasis/kolazo (Greek) – removed; separated[25]

The word used in English translations of the Bible, *punish*, conveys an external infliction of negative consequences, while the original words, *avon* (Hebrew) and *kolasis/kolazo* (Greek) convey internal, self-imposed consequences (i.e. carrying the weight of guilt/shame) and natural consequences (i.e. being estranged).

There is no fear in love. But perfect love drives out fear, because fear has to do with ~~punishment~~ *bearing one's own iniquity, carrying guilt, feeling shame, being estranged.*
(1 John 4:18)

Jesus came to take our place, to bear our iniquities, to carry our guilt, to free us from shame, and to reunite us with our Father, and the literal translation conveys that truth perfectly.

The thing is, instant obedience and thoughtless compliance based on fear of punishment will always be an external and temporary 'fix' for behavior issues, as evidenced by the increasingly defiant and disconnected Israelite nation in the Old Testament, while thoughtful consideration and cooperation are internal, a heart-deep and soul-to-soul connection inspired by compassion, respect, and communication. Consider this passage from *The Gentle Parent: Positive, Practical, Effective Discipline*:

> Someone once wrote, "Obedience is doing what you're told, no matter what's right. Morality is doing what's

right, no matter what you're told." History preserved the quote, but not the source with any credibility, but it's a wise statement nonetheless.

Growing children with an inner compass that guides their steps toward kindness and compassion and generosity of spirit is far, far and away superior to training children to operate on automatic pilot. Parents often focus so much time and energy on trying to make their children obey in the small moments of life that they forget to step back and take a panoramic view of how their parenting choices may affect their children's life course.

'Instant obedience' is the new catch-phrase in many popular parenting articles and books, but the reality is that, while instant obedience may be convenient for parents in the moment, it can have powerful negative impacts on the adults their children will become.

Training children into instant obedience is the equivalent of disabling their inner guidance system and strapping on a remote-controlled rocket. The end result may be adults who are easily controlled by others or adults who are deeply divided, constantly fighting the external controls, but hampered by an erratic, immature inner compass that never had the chance to develop properly.

Equipping children with a healthy, well-functioning internal guidance system, an inner compass, takes time, patience, and self-control on the part of the parents. Certainly not a convenient alternative! While it may not be convenient to slow down our hectic life pace and really connect with our children, it's that connection that enables their internal guidance system to come online. While taking the time to really communicate may be a sacrifice, it's in that communication that the directions on their inner guidance system are set. And, while working cooperatively with our children may take more time and effort, the fact is that inviting cooperation rather than forcing compliance raises leaders instead of reaping followers.

Clearly, teaching our children to control themselves is far more effective in the long-term than trying to control our children, but how, specifically, can we go about equipping them with those all-important internal controls?

- Model instead of manipulate.
- Invite instead of intimidate.
- Support instead of shame.
- Encourage instead of enrage.
- Teach instead of threaten.
- Listen instead of lecture.
- Help instead of hurt.
- Parent instead of punish.

Instant obedience and mindless compliance are poor goals, indeed, when raising children. A thoughtfully questioning, passionately curious, and humorously resourceful child who delights in inventing 'compromises' and who endlessly pushes the boundaries tends to become a thoughtful, passionate, resourceful adult who will change the world rather than being changed by the world.

These are simple truths, and yet their effects are profound when we embrace them and incorporate them into our parenting. Connection, Communication, and Cooperation, the Three C's of gentle parenting, are powerful and effective tools in guiding our children toward self-control to help them learn to steer their own ships, and, if we are to be fishers of men, then isn't a ship headed out to sea exactly what each of us should be, anyway? Instead of mooring our children to the shore, let's sail alongside them in the sometimes calm, sometimes stormy, but always glorious sea of life, keeping them sheltered on our leeward side until they are ready to sail alone.

"For I am the Lord your God who takes hold of your right hand
and says to you, Do not fear; I will help you."
Isaiah 41:13

Chapter 8

Did Jesus have a Temper Tantrum?

*"Jesus entered the temple courts and drove out all who were
buying and selling there. He overturned the tables of the money
changers and the benches of those selling doves. "It is written,"
he said to them, "'My house will be called a house of prayer
but you are making it a den of robbers.'"*
Matthew 21:12-13

*Temper tantrum: (n.) a loss of mental balance or composure,
esp. an outburst of anger or irritation[26]*

It may seem a bit disrespectful to label Jesus' takedown in the
temple courtyard as a temper tantrum, but according to the
dictionary definition of a tantrum, that would be an accurate
designation. He acted out his overwhelming emotions by
flipping over tables and throwing chairs and chasing people
away in a God-sized, epic tantrum that must have shocked the
religious to their core and rocked the pharisaical back on their
heels.

So what's the deal? Are temper tantrums signs of a child's
sinful, selfish nature, as the child-training set are so quick to
accuse, or are they normal expressions of overwhelming
emotions? Let's see what the child-trainers have to say:

> *"A temper tantrum is an absolute rejection of parental
> authority. Parents should isolate the child (with a
> promise of consequences), then follow through with
> chastisement [spanking] after the child settles down."[27]
> (Gary Ezzo, Growing Kid's God's Way)*

> *"...tantrums are a form of challenging behavior that
> can be eliminated by one or more appropriate
> spankings.(p. 108)"[28] (Dr. James Dobson, The New
> Dare to Discipline)*

"A seven-month-old boy had, upon failing to get his way, stiffened, clenched his fists, bared his toothless gums and called down damnation on the whole place. At a time like that, the angry expression on a baby's face can resemble that of one instigating a riot. The young mother, wanting to do the right thing, stood there in helpless consternation, apologetically shrugged her shoulders and said, "What can I do?" My incredulous nine-year-old whipped back, "Switch him." The mother responded, "I can't, he's too little." With the wisdom of a veteran who had been on the little end of the switch, my daughter answered, "If he is old enough to pitch a fit, he is old enough to be spanked.(p. 79)"[17] (Michael Pearl, To Train Up a Child)

"If your child is still angry, it's time for another round. 'Daddy has spanked you, but you are not sweet enough yet. We are going to have to go back upstairs for another spanking.'"[4] (Tedd Tripp, Shepherding a Child's Heart)

So, what do you think, parents? Is acting out of overwhelming emotions a sin that must be punished as the child-trainers claim or is it normal human behavior? Is there even such a thing as *normal* human behavior, or is human behavior itself sinful by its very nature? Is having overwhelming emotions, in and of itself, a sin?

Sin, Biblically speaking, is acting outside of God's nature. Since Jesus is God in the flesh, he was clearly acting *within* God's nature at all times, even though he was also fully human. So, Jesus' actions and his human behaviors, his *normal human behaviors*, all fell within the boundaries of God's nature and therefore were and are not sinful.

Let's go back to Jesus and breakdown the takedown in the temple. He was angry. He toppled tables. He threw things. He chased people away. But Jesus was and is sinless, so clearly being angry, being overwhelmed by big emotions, and acting on those emotions are not sins, in and of themselves.

When does acting on emotions become sinful, then? The answer lies in Ephesians 4:26-27, *"In your anger do not sin: Do not let the sun go down while you are still angry, and do not give the devil a foothold."* Note that it doesn't say, "Getting angry is a sin."

Emotions can *lead to* sin when they remain unsettled, are left to burrow deeply into our hearts and take root, and when we subsequently respond with spite, bitterness, vengeance, or rage.

As parents, then, how can we help our children when they are overwhelmed by their emotions, when they tantrum and cry and act out their big feelings? Does it make sense to expect them to cope with their big emotions alone or to suppress their emotions so they remain unsettled?

Of course not. Our children need us to parent them, not punish them.

> *"God is our refuge and strength,*
> *an ever-present help in times of trouble."(Psalm 46:1b)*

Just as God is *"our refuge and strength"* and *"an ever-present help"* that is what we need to be for our children, to reflect the heart of our Father to our own little ones. We can help them to process their emotions. We can work with them to resolve their problems. And we can equip them with the life skills they'll need to handle their emotions on their own when they grow into adulthood.

As you read on, remind yourself that having emotions is not a sin and needing help processing those emotions is a normal part of childhood:

> When a little person feels frustrated, overwhelmed, or just plain old out-of-sorts (read: tantrum time!), it's tempting for parents to focus on correction rather than connection. But when children are intensely stressed, the prefrontal cortex of the brain, which in early childhood is an underdeveloped, mushy grey sponge waiting to be formed, is flooded with cortisol, the 'stress hormone.' The result is what is known as the

fight-freeze-or-flight syndrome in which higher brain functions (learning, reason, self-control) are markedly hampered and lower brain functions (instinct, physical reactions) take over. This is an in-built survival mechanism that gradually comes under conscious control through years of growth in a safe and supportive environment. Interestingly, it is theorized that this underdeveloped 'sponginess' is why small children are able to learn new languages more quickly than older children and adults. They are, in a very literal way, absorbing information raw, unhampered by the processing and reason of a more mature brain.[29]

Expecting young children to have the maturity and self-control to overcome this God-given survival instinct is unrealistic. Threatening, punishing, or even reasoning with them while their higher brain functions are suppressed is futile and actually just adds more stress to the situation (more stress = fuel on the tantrum-fire!).

What they really need is help…

- First, help coping with their big emotions

- Then, help reconnecting with their source of safety and security (you!)

- And last, help processing the problem that sent them into a maelstrom of emotion in the first place.

Punishing them, yelling at them, sending them to their room, or putting them in time-out disconnects them even further from their source of security and not only delays a resolution of the issue, but misses an opportunity to equip them with the tools they need to handle future problems.

This is where the Three C's of gentle discipline come into play:

Connection:

- Remaining present and supportive until they are able to calm down enough to accept your help

- Drawing them close when they're ready (time-in)

Communication:

- Validating their emotions by labeling them and empathizing (i.e. "You're sad because we have to leave the park. I'm sad, too. The park is fun!")

- Offering words to help them express their frustrations using reflective language (i.e. "It's hard to do things we don't like, isn't it?")

Cooperation:

- Helping them move on by redirecting their attention to the future (i.e. "When we get home we're going to make a snack. Would you like grapes or bananas today?")

- Modeling coping skills and self-control by calming your own reaction to their meltdown and helping them process their big emotions

These are all ways of reconnecting with your toddler or preschooler to help them successfully navigate their present difficulty as well as to cope with difficulties they're confronted with in the future.

One effective tool for use in helping little ones cope with big emotions is a Calm-Me-Jar made from small, round, plastic bottles such as Aquapod™ water bottles. They are perfect for small hands to shake and manhandle to their heart's content.

To make your own Calm-Me-Jar, fill up a plastic water bottle with warm water and basic craft glitter glue in whatever color you like. You can add some extra glitter and a drop of food coloring to customize your glitter jar to your child's tastes, and then when you have the look you want, be sure to hot glue the top on to prevent spills.

When my little ones have meltdowns, or, if I can catch it, before they reach that point, I pull out one of the Calm-Me-Jars and shake it up and just let them hold it while I hold them (when they are ready to be held) and talk or sing quietly. When I feel their body relaxing and their breathing slow down, I might say something like, "It's sad when we can't have a toy, isn't it?" or whatever else will reflect what they seem to be unable to express.

When an older preschooler or early elementary-aged child has a meltdown, or, again, before if I can catch it, I first connect, "I'm here. I can see you're upset. How can I help?" and listen as they try to verbalize their feelings. If they're having trouble with the words, instead of immediately supplying the words for them, I'll offer them a Calm-Me-Jar and ask if they'd like to show me how they're feeling. They will often shake the Calm-Me-Jar vigorously while jumping up and down and twisting all around, which is a great physical outlet for their intense feelings. I watch until I see their movements slowing and their breathing evening out, and when they've calmed just enough to hear me, I quietly talk them through the calming process, "Look at all that fairy dust bouncing around like crazy! I bet that's how it feels inside when you're so upset. Look at how it's starting to slow down and settle to the bottom. If we breathe really slowly, we can feel ourselves settling like the fairy dust. Want to try it with me?" Then, if there are any behavior issues we need to address, we'll work through those afterward when they're calm, connected, and capable of interacting and understanding.

Here's an example of how Calm-Me-Jars are helpful in 'listening between the lines' to my children's behavior so I can meet them where they are and help them process their big feelings:

> My five-year-old is a tiny girl with BIG emotions, and she really likes using Calm-Me-Jars to work through her feelings. We've put several together such as a silvery one she named *Goodnight Moon*, a light blue one she named *Nemo Under the Sea*, a pink one she named *Hello Kitty Princess Ballerina*, and a dark blue one she named *Starry, Starry Night*. When she is mad at one of her siblings, she'll often bring me one of her Calm-Me-Jars (*Goodnight Moon* is a favorite in the evening!) and work out some of her upset physically by shaking the jar like crazy while she jumps up and down and tells me how mad she is. When she's a bit calmer, we'll have a little cuddle and watch the glitter settle while saying goodnight to the moon, all the furniture, and whatever other silliness we come up with until she's calm. If there's a discipline issue or she needs some help working things out with a sibling, we'll work through it at that point because I know that's when she can hear me and really process what I'm saying. If she chooses *Starry, Starry Night* we might sing *Twinkle, Twinkle Little Star* or step outside and see if there are any stars out yet. If she decides on *Hello Kitty Princess Ballerina* she'll often dance her frustrations away while shaking her Calm-Me-Jar. And if she picks out *Nemo Under the Sea* we'll 'speak whale' like Dory from *Finding Nemo*[8] or we'll make fishy faces at each other until we're both giggling.

As you can see, my feisty little girl's choice of Calm-Me-Jar shows me what she needs to do to work through her emotions of the moment, whether it's to act things out physically in acceptable ways or to connect through song or through silliness.

The key is being in tune with your little one enough to understand their personality and work with it instead of against it. My five-year-old is spunky and silly, so having a long, serious talk would drive her crazy and accomplish nothing. We quickly decide together how she'll approach whatever the problem was the next time she encounters it, and then she's ready to move on, whereas when some of my older ones were little they really liked to talk things through (and still do!). My toddler, on the other hand, doesn't have tantrums because that simply isn't part of her own unique personality, but she's still fascinated by her Calm-Me-Jar and loves to sit with me and watch the "pintess faywe dut" ("princess fairy dust") glitter settle when she's feeling a bit cranky or out-of-sorts.

Remember, there is no cure for tantrums because they are simply a normal result of a normal developmental stage of childhood. Trying to avoid tantrum triggers (tiredness, hunger, overstimulation, etc.) is always a good first step, along with remaining in-tune, responsive, and available, but when all else fails and a tantrum does occur, reacting with an adult tantrum is tantamount to throwing fuel on a toddler-tantrum-fire. So instead of losing it when your little one loses it, take an adult time-out, breathe deeply to gain control of your own emotions, and then grab the Three C's of gentle discipline from your parenting toolbox and work with your child, not against them. (*Two Thousand Kisses a Day: Gentle Parenting Through the Ages and Stages*)

Reactors react to a crisis with a meltdown. Responders respond to a crisis with help. To raise a mature, stable adult, be a first responder, not a nuclear reactor!

> *"God is our refuge and our strength,*
> *an ever-present help in times of trouble"*
> *Psalm 46:1b*

Chapter 9

Grace has a Face

*"Let the little children come to me,
and do not hinder them, for the kingdom of God
belongs to such as these"
Luke 18:16b*

....

*The tiny girl stood timidly at the top of the stairs, her
small face anxious as she called out in toddler-eze,
"Dada, do you comin?"*

*The man sitting in front of a small group of church
leaders gathered in his living room grimaced. "Oops!
Forgot I told her I'd be up in five minutes to tuck her in
and say her prayers." He shook his head and glanced
around the room with a self-deprecating grin, "I forget
my promises more often than not, unfortunately.
Hazards of a busy schedule, I guess." He sighed, "I
told her to wait in her bed for me. Now I have to go
spank her, poor thing. It'll be the third time today. I
wish parenting was easier."*

*An older man stood and gestured to the others in the
room to gather around the man. "Let's pray for
strength for our brother to fulfill his fatherly duties
unwaveringly and cheerfully."*

*As the church leaders joined hands and prayed, the
lone woman in the group stood aside. She looked from
the tiny face still peering down through the stair railing
to the gathering of adults solemnly praying over the
little girl's father, her heart racing as a flood of
memories darkened her mind.*

The prayer ended, and the father started up the steps.

The woman's breath caught in her throat as a smile lit the toddler's face when she saw her daddy approaching, her little hand reaching out trustingly to take his as he led her back to her bedroom. The bedroom door closed and silent moments passed, then muffled thwaps and cries of pain split the silence. A few minutes later the door opened, letting the sound of the small girl's sobs drift clearly down the stairs before they were muffled again as the father emerged, his own eyes wet with tears, and closed the door softly behind him. The father hastily wiped his eyes, then rejoined the group downstairs.

The church leaders patted the father on the back, reassuring him that everyone made mistakes and forgot things at times, so he shouldn't feel guilty about forgetting his promise to his child. They offered a few pieces of sage advice about securing a child's unquestioning obedience with consistent punishment and reminded him to be unwavering in its application.

Then they returned to their meeting, trying to come up with a church program to share the unconditional love and freely given grace of their Heavenly Father with the wounded, the broken, the lost. The woman excused herself, and as she moved toward the front door she heard one man propose that they call the new program, 'Grace is for Everyone.'

She barely made it to her car before collapsing into soul-shaking sobs.

The woman had been that little girl, once upon a life-time ago. Now she was the wounded, the broken, the lost. Her childhood wounds so often gaped and grasped, sucking any momentary joy from her heart and unexpectedly festering into flashes of anger that shocked her when they suddenly surfaced. Her broken trust shattered her relationship with her heavenly Daddy again and again as she grappled to understand and accept an unconditional love that she had never experienced at the hands of her earthly father. Her way seemed littered with roadblocks and pitfalls as she wandered in the darkness of a lost world, terrified that she would fail and be lost forever.

With a shuddering breath, the woman started her car and drove away, her heart aching for a tiny girl sobbing herself to sleep alone in a dark room and for an adult who would soon be doing the same thing.

*This is a true story. Some details have been changed for confidentiality.

How much different might it have been if the story had gone this way, instead:

The tiny girl stood timidly at the top of the stairs, her small face anxious as she called out in toddler-eze, "Dada, do you comin?"

The man sitting in front of a small group of church leaders gathered in his living room grimaced. "Oops! Forgot I told her I'd be up in five minutes to tuck her in and say her prayers." He shook his head and glanced around the room with a self-deprecating grin, "I forget my promises more often than not, unfortunately. Hazards of a busy schedule, I guess." He sighed, "I told her to wait in her bed for me. Now I have to go apologize to her, poor thing. It'll be the third time I've had to apologize for dropping the ball today. I wish parenting was easier."

An older man grinned and said, "Go take care of your little girl. We can wait."

The father started up the stairs.

As the church leaders chatted while they waited for the man to return, the lone woman in the group sat silently. She looked at the tiny face still peering down through the stair railing, and her heart raced as a flood of memories darkened her mind.

The woman's breath caught in her throat as a smile lit the toddler's face when she saw her daddy approaching, her little hand reaching out trustingly to take his as he led her back to her bedroom. The bedroom door closed and silent moments passed, then muffled giggles wafted through the silence. A few minutes later the door opened, letting the sound of the small girl whispering, "Dood night, Dada!" drift clearly down the stairs as the father emerged, his eyes wet with tears, and closed the door softly behind him. The father hastily wiped his eyes, then rejoined the group downstairs.

As the father sat down, he cleared his throat, a bemused smile lighting his face. "I guess that's why Jesus said, 'Let the little children come to me,'" he said, "because children are so good at giving unconditional love and forgiving and trusting. No matter how many times I disappoint that little girl, no matter how many promises I break, she always forgives me and trusts me completely."

The church leaders smiled and nodded, reassuring him that everyone made mistakes and forgot things at times, so he shouldn't feel guilty about forgetting his promise to his child, after all, he was only human. They offered a few pieces of advice about juggling a busy schedule with children and reminded him that family always comes first.

Then they returned to their meeting, trying to come up with a church program to share the unconditional love and freely given grace of their Heavenly Father with the wounded, the broken, and the lost, both in their church and in their community. One leader mentioned, "I think that beautiful analogy about your daughter you just shared would make a perfect starting point for our program." As the others in the room nodded their approval, someone proposed that they call the new program, 'Grace is for Everyone.'

A few minutes later, the meeting broke up and everyone made their way home, but the woman sat in the dark driveway in her car with tears running down her cheeks.

She had been that little girl, once upon a life-time ago, waiting...hoping for a father's love, but she had never received the compassion and humanity that she had witnessed that evening. Her childhood wounds so often gaped and grasped, sucking any momentary joy from her heart and unexpectedly festering into flashes of anger that shocked her when they suddenly surfaced. Her broken trust shattered her relationship with her heavenly Daddy again and again as she grappled to understand and accept an unconditional love that she had never experienced at the hands of her earthly father. Her way seemed littered with roadblocks and pitfalls as she wandered in the darkness of a lost world, terrified that she would fail and be lost forever.

With a slight smile, the woman started her car and drove away, her heart swelling with the unfamiliar feelings of hope and healing as she thought of a tiny girl peacefully sleeping in the safety of her father's love and of an adult who might actually be doing the same thing for the first time in as long as she could remember.

Here's the thing, parents, either grace is sufficient for all or it is sufficient for none. There is no in-between. You are your children's first taste of God, their first understanding of love, their first vision of grace. How you treat them in that capacity will inevitably affect their relationship with Christ. Choose love, because he is Love in the flesh. Choose gentleness, because he is the Gentle Shepherd. Choose grace, because he died so that you could.

Grace has a face…

It's yours.

"Whatever you have learned or received or heard from me, or seen in me—put it into practice."
Philippians 4:9

Chapter 10

Don't Train a Child

"Therefore be imitators of God as dear children.
And walk in love, as Christ also has loved us and given Himself
for us, an offering and a sacrifice to God"
Ephesians 5:1-2

Parents worldwide have one thing in common…a deep, heartfelt desire to raise their children 'right,' to do their best to raise healthy, responsible, happy people. And, again almost universally, those parents look to others to help guide them on their parenting journey. Sometimes they look to their own family or to close friends, but often they seek out parenting guides, trusting that what they read in a book from a parenting 'expert' must be right…right?

What they don't realize is that anyone can write a parenting book, and it's often the expertise in marketing rather than in parenting that sells the most books. Here are excerpts and quotes from some of today's most widely read and trusted self-proclaimed parenting experts:

> *"After ten acts of stubborn defiance, followed by ten*
> *switchings, he surrendered his will to one higher than*
> *himself." (about whipping a 15 month old) …"Don't*
> *wait until they are one year old to start training.*
> *Rebellion and self-will should be broken in the six-*
> *month-old when it first appears" …never show mercy.*
> *One squeak of a scream gets a switching." (about*
> *whipping a 3-year-old) …"For young children,*
> *especially during the first year, the rod is used as a*
> *training tool. You use something small and light to get*
> *the child's attention and to reinforce your command.*
> *One or two light licks on the bare legs or arms will*
> *cause a child to stop in his tracks and regard your*
> *commands. A 12-inch piece of weed eater chord(sic)*
> *works well as a beginner rod. It will fit in your purse or*

pocket. Later, a plumber's supply line is a good spanking tool...A baby needs to be trained all day, everyday."[17] (Michael Pearl, To Train up a Child)

"Pain is a marvelous purifier...It is not necessary to beat the child into submission; a little bit of pain goes a long way for a young child. However, the spanking should be of sufficient magnitude to cause the child to cry genuinely... Real crying usually lasts two minutes or less, but may continue for five. After that point, the child is merely complaining... I would require him to stop the protest crying, usually by offering him a little more of whatever caused the original tears."[30] (Dr. James Dobson, Dare to Discipline)

"Even at mealtime, be looking for training opportunities in order to avoid retraining. Don't allow poor eating habits– such as fingers in the mouth, playing with food, and spitting out food–to become a normal pattern of your child's behavior. It only means correcting the child at a later date"[31] (Ezzo, Babywise II, p. 44) ..."Chastisement [spanking] is the price paid to remove the guilt thus free the child from his burden. If the parents do not remove the guilt, the child lives under the weight of sin."[27] (Gary Ezzo, Growing Kids God's Way, p. 212)

"A parent must recognize and see clearly that Biblically beating his child sensitizes that child not only to the fact of sin but also to its ugliness. In addition, the child will see that the penalty must always be paid when we sin...The one who does not Biblically beat his child, in a loving and consistent way, in a very real sense predisposes that child for hell and even has a very direct part in sending him there."[6] (Ronald E. Williams, The Correction and Salvation of Children)

"The rod is a parent, in faith toward God and faithfulness toward his or her children, undertaking the responsibility of careful, timely, measured and controlled use of physical punishment to underscore the importance of obeying God...If you fail to spank, you

> *fail to take God's Word seriously. You are saying you
> do not believe what the Bible teaches about the import
> of these issues. You are saying that you do not love
> your child enough to do the painful things that God has
> called you to."[4] (Tedd Tripp, Shepherding a Child's
> Heart)*

These self-styled parenting 'experts' and others mandate strict, unemotional behavioral controls, often enforced punitively, stemming from a shared core ideology that children need to be trained…trained to self-soothe, trained to sleep alone, trained to play independently, trained to instantly obey.

Much of the root of the idea that children need to be trained comes from the Old Testament verse, *"Train up a child in the way he should go, and when he is old he will not depart from it." (Proverbs 22:6)*

The word translated *train up* in that verse is the Hebrew word *chanak/chanokh* which translated literally means '*to dedicate or to initiate.*'[1,2,3] To dedicate means to *'commit to a special use'* and *'to focus on a specific purpose.'* To initiate means to *'introduce to, create an appetite or a taste for'* and *'to set on the path.'* In every other Old Testament usage of *chanak/chanokh* it is translated *'to dedicate or to initiate'* except for the 'train up a child' verse.

Thus, the verse literally reads…

"~~Train up~~ Introduce a child to/set a child on the path in the way he should go, and when he is old he will not depart from it." (Proverbs 22:6)

That verse, coupled with a handful of others such as the 'spare the rod' verses (see Chapter Eleven), has led to an entire parenting paradigm based on Old Testament practices of rigid expectations and harsh consequences, purported to be 'God's way.' Parents are often bullied or intimidated into following these strict parenting models with dire predictions of raising 'brats' or rebels and threats of being in opposition to 'God's will.'

Incidentally, it's interesting to note how just as a child begins to develop the cognitive ability to have impulse control and forethought, their 'need' to be spanked begins to drastically decrease. The child-trainers say this is because their early training is paying off. Brain science says this is because they are developing at a normal rate.[32]

Now, before we examine the supposed correlation of strict, punishment-based parenting to positive parenting outcomes and gentle, connection-based parenting to negative parenting outcomes, let's take a quick look at the God of the Old Testament…that seemingly distant, unreachable, merciless, commanding, harshly punishing image being touted as the parenting model we must follow.

Old Testament=Punishment-based Parenting

In the Old Testament, the Bible prescribed rigid do's and don'ts along with decisive and harsh consequences for anything less than strict obedience. As time went on and the people rebelled (Wait, rebelled? Strict, punishent-based parenting with harsh punitive consequences resulted in rebellion instead of obedience?) more and more regulations were layered on the Israelites along with commensurate penalties.

The result? More rebellion!

No matter how many rules, how many threats, how much follow-thru on punishments that were meted out, punishment-based parenting just flat out didn't work, even for God. Of course, he already knew it wouldn't work.

So why did he do it?

Well, God doesn't do anything arbitrarily. He was showing us something and using a big, yellow highlighter called 'The Law' to do it…

"YOU HAVE FALLEN AND YOU CAN'T GET UP!"

Sin entered the world when humans first had the thought planted in their minds…"You don't need God. You can BE God!"…and humans took the bait and were separated from their Father.

In the Old Testament, God used that big yellow highlighter, the Law, to show humans that they aren't God and can't work their way or earn their way or find any other way to be God or to find God on their own, period. The Old Testament proved that definitively. And the Law, with its punishment-based parenting, didn't bring obedience or peace or reconciliation. It brought only rebellion, suffering, exile.

So, God set out to reconnect with his children.

And how did he do it? Gentle parenting…

New Testament=Connection-based Parenting

God stepped right down in the flesh for skin-to-skin (à la kangaroo care!) time with his children. In Jesus, he lived and slept and walked with his children day and night, always available, meeting every need whether it was food, healing, guidance, or comfort.

God didn't parent his children from a distance. He didn't force separation on them. He didn't respond to their sin in cold blood. In fact, he did just the opposite. He closed the distance, bridged the separation man's sin had created, and poured out his own blood to atone for his children so they could be close to him forever.

So…the purportedly tyrannical parent of the Old Testament who supposedly commands us to rigidly train and harshly punish our children is actually, himself, a gentle Parent!

> *"As a mother comforts her child, so will I comfort you."*
> *(Isaiah 66:13)*

Punishment-based vs Connection-based Parenting Outcomes

As to the supposed correlation of strict, punishment-based parenting to positive parenting outcomes and gentle, connection-based parenting to negative parenting outcomes, here are some interesting studies…

> "As 5-year-olds, the children who had been spanked were more likely than the non-spanked to be defiant, demand immediate satisfaction of their wants and needs, become frustrated easily, have temper tantrums and lash out physically against other people or animals"[33](Time, Physical Punishment Increases Aggression in Children)

> "Physical punishment is also associated with a variety of mental health problems, such as depression, anxiety and use of drugs and alcohol"[34] (Science Daily, Canadian Medical Association Journal: Long-term Negative Effects of Physical Punishment)

> "IQs of children ages 2 to 4 who were not spanked were 5 points higher four years later than the IQs of those who were spanked"[35] (Science Daily, Research Shows Children Who Are Spanked Have Lower IQ's)

> "Dr. Brazy at Duke University and Ludington-Hoe and colleagues at Case Western University showed in 2 separate studies how prolonged crying in infants causes increased blood pressure in the brain, elevates stress hormones, obstructs blood from draining out of the brain, and decreases oxygenation to the brain. They concluded that caregivers should answer cries swiftly, consistently, and comprehensively."[36] (Dr. William Sears: Studies on the Effects of Excessive/Prolonged Crying in Infancy)

> "Dr. Allan Schore (1996), of the UCLA School of Medicine has demonstrated that the stress hormone cortisol can damage nerve connections in significant areas of the infant's brain. His research suggests that not only does stress damage connections in these areas of the infant's brain but when the areas of the infant's brain responsible for bonding, emotional control, and

attachment are not nurtured in a healthy way, those
areas remain undeveloped or underdeveloped"[37]
(Cambridge Journal, Studies on the Effects of
Prolonged Crying in Infancy)

Listen, parents, to your heart. Listen to your children. Treat your children how you, yourself, want to be treated. Read parenting books, blogs, articles, etc. if you need guidance, but do so with discernment. You are your children's parents. No one on earth loves them or knows them like you do. You'll make mistakes, for sure. We all do. But if you learn from those mistakes and do better next time…well, that's the stuff of life, isn't it?

"The Lord is good to all; he has compassion on
all he has made."
Psalm 145:9

Chapter 11

Spare the Rod: The Heart of the Matter

"Your rod and your staff, they comfort me…"
Psalm 23:4b

One of the hot-button issues when it comes to discipline and children is, of course, spanking, and the more Christian and conservative the audience, the more hot the debate becomes. And yet there are *no verses* in the New Testament that support spanking, smacking, whipping, or otherwise hitting children.

In the Old Testament there are a total of five verses that have been interpreted to encourage, or even command, the use of physical punishment on children. All five of those verses are in the book of Proverbs. The word 'proverb' in the original Hebrew text is *mashal*[1,2,3] and defined as a parable, prophetic and figurative discourse, symbolic poem, pithy maxim (i.e. a collection of wise metaphors and adages).[38]

Of interest is that ancient Hebrew had many words for children, each denoting a specific stage of childhood and many a specific gender:

> *yeled* or *yaldah* - newborn boy or girl
>
> *yonek* or *yanak* - nursling baby
>
> *olel* – nursling baby who also eats food (translated 'young child' in Lamentations 4:4 KJV)
>
> *gamal* - weaned child (around 3-4 years old)
>
> *taph* - young child, one who still clings to their mother
>
> *elem* or *almah* - firm and strong, older child

na'ar (masc.) or *na'arah* (fem.) - independent child, young adult child (includes older adolescents and young adults)[1,2,3]

The word translated 'child' and 'children' in those Old Testament rod verses is *na'ar*, which when literally translated, means 'young man.'

Let's look, also, at the words translated 'discipline' and 'punish' and 'rod' and others:

The word *muwcar* is translated 'discipline' and means, literally, 'verbal instruction and teaching.' In Hebrew culture *muwcar* was vernacular for 'let us reason with one another' implying a mutual discussion for learning purposes. And *towkechah* is translated 'reprove' or 'rebuke' but also means 'reason with, convince, prove, persuade.' Neither of these words means to physically punish in any way, shape, or form.

The word *nakah* is translated 'punish' in most English translations of the Bible, though its literal translation is 'beat' as in "The sun beat down on his head," implying a constant presence; or 'hit' as when beating back an enemy or punishing a slave or criminal; or 'smite or smitten' which can mean 'hit or trigger the conscience' or 'be favorably impressed, enticed, or entranced' as in, "He was smitten with the idea of a new bicycle."[1,2,3]

The word *shebet* is translated 'rod' and means, literally, 'shepherd's crook' and, in Hebrew culture, was a means not only of guiding and protecting sheep, but also a symbol of leadership. The markings on the head of the *shebet* often identified the head of a family or tribe, letting everyone know who to go to for guidance and protection. The *shebet*, then, denotes wisdom, leadership, and protection. [1,2,3]

The word *muwth* is translated 'die' and has several meanings related to death including 'to follow a path of destruction.'[1,2,3]

The word *'ivveleth* is translated 'foolishness' but also means 'inexperience, naivety, silliness.'[1,2,3]

And, finally, the Hebrew word *sane* is translated 'hate' and yet means 'does not love' or 'does not choose or show a preference for.'[1,2,3]

When we read the five 'rod' verses with the literal translations of the words above, the meanings become more clear.

So Proverbs 13:24 reads:

> *"He who spares his ~~rod~~ wisdom, leadership, protection ~~hates~~ does not love, does not choose or show a preference for his son, but he who loves him ~~disciplines~~ offers verbal instruction and teaching to him promptly."*

Proverbs 22:15 reads:

> *"~~Foolishness~~ Naivety, silliness, inexperience is bound up in the heart of a ~~child~~ young man; ~~the rod of correction~~ wisdom, leadership, protection will drive it far from him."*

Proverbs 29:15 reads:

> *"~~The rod~~ Wisdom, leadership, protection and ~~rebuke~~ reasoning with, convincing, proving, persuading give wisdom, but a ~~child~~ young man left to himself brings shame to his mother."*

And, the last two 'rod' verses, found in Proverbs 23:12-26 read:

> *"Apply your heart to instruction and your ears to words of knowledge.*
>
> *Do not withhold ~~discipline~~ verbal instruction and teaching, reasoning together from a ~~child~~ young man;*
>
> *if you ~~punish~~ guide, trigger his conscience, favorably impress, entice/entrance them with ~~the rod~~ wisdom, leadership, protection, they will not ~~die~~ follow a path of destruction.*

~~Punish~~ Guide, trigger his conscience, favorably
impress, entice/entrance them with ~~the rod~~ wisdom,
leadership, protection and save them from ~~death~~
following a path of destruction.

My son, if your heart is wise, then my heart will be glad
indeed;

my inmost being will rejoice when your lips speak what
is right.

Do not let your heart envy sinners, but always be
zealous for the fear of the Lord.

There is surely a future hope for you, and your hope
will not be cut off.

Listen, my son, and be wise, and set your heart on the
right path:

Do not join those who drink too much wine or gorge
themselves on meat,

for drunkards and gluttons become poor, and
drowsiness clothes them in rags.

Listen to your father, who gave you life, and do not
despise your mother when she is old.

Buy the truth and do not sell it—wisdom, instruction
and insight as well.

The father of a righteous ~~child~~ young man has great
joy; a man who fathers a wise son rejoices in him.

May your father and mother rejoice; may she who gave
you birth be joyful!

My son, give me your heart and let your eyes delight in
my ways."

Such a beautiful image of a father tenderly and diligently sharing
his wisdom with his son, isn't it? Clearly, applying these
scriptures to small children is not in line with a literal
interpretation. It actually makes more sense to apply them to the
disciples, which is exactly what Jesus does with his twelve
'sons.'

Beyond translations and interpretations, though, and of far greater import, what seems to get lost in the spanking debate is that Jesus brought grace and mercy as his methods and message for a reason. The purpose of the law in the Old Testament was to highlight the need for a Savior because humans simply cannot live perfectly.

Jesus came to fulfill the outward requirements of the law that highlighted man's sins and replace them with an inner heart change. He demonstrated in many ways that the law (outer governance and control through fear of punishment) was no longer to be a rigid yoke with its heavy burden of cleansing and rituals and sacrifices and punishments, but instead was to be a kingdom of the heart, of mercy not sacrifice, because the sacrifice was Himself.

Jesus stopped the people from stoning the prostitute (John 8:2-11) which was a requirement in the Old Testament. (Deuteronomy 22:21-22)

Jesus healed people and traveled on the Sabbath (Matthew 12:1-14) which was punishable by death in the Old Testament. (Exodus 31:14-17 and Numbers 15:32-36)

Jesus consorted with 'sinners' and ate with them (Luke 15:1-2) despite the admonitions in Proverbs 13:20. (the same book in the Bible with the 'rod' scriptures)

Jesus showed again and again that if we accept him as our Savior, we are called to be *"ministers of a new covenant—not of the letter but of the Spirit; for the letter kills, but the Spirit gives life." (2 Corinthians 3:6)*

We accept that Jesus brought a new and better way, a way of the heart, *"Not on tablets of stone but on tablets of human hearts." (2 Corinthians 3:3b),* but don't seem to want to acknowledge that better way with our children.

We accept God's grace and forgiveness for ourselves, but often don't share those gifts with, and model them for, our children.

But *we* are our children's first taste of God. Is it any wonder people have such a hard time understanding grace and mercy and unconditional love when they may not have been taught those things by their earthly parents and don't exercise them with their own children?

Through Jesus' sacrifice, he tore open the veil dividing man from God and brought a new kingdom, a kingdom of inner governance through the Holy Spirit whose fruit is "peace, patience, kindness, goodness, faithfulness, gentleness, and self-control." Nowhere does Jesus say to follow him *except* when it comes to our children. He doesn't say to offer grace and mercy and forgiveness to everyone *except* our children. The Bible doesn't tell us to show the fruit of the Spirit to everyone *except* our children.

If we truly believe that, based on five verses in the Old Testament with disputable translations and debatable interpretations, we are being disobedient to God's commands if we don't spank our children, then we must take that belief and walk it out fully.

In other words, if we must obey that supposed command, then we must obey all the other commands such as,,,

- an *"eye for an eye"* (Exodus 21:24) and stoning adulterers (Leviticus 20:10) …but didn't Jesus bring forgiveness?

- we shouldn't feed the homeless because *"if a man doesn't work, neither shall he eat"* (2 Thessalonians 3:10) …but aren't we supposed to be the heart and hands of Jesus?

- we shouldn't give Christmas shoeboxes to prisoners' children because *"the sins of the father are visited on the children"* (Exodus 20:5) …but isn't the *"kingdom of heaven made up of such as these?"* (Matthew 19:14)

My point is summed up in this verse:

"For whoever keeps the whole law and yet stumbles at just one point is guilty of breaking all of it." (James 2:10)

In other words, if you feel bound by those five verses, then you must be bound by all.

If you truly believe that those five verses have been interpreted correctly and that "spare the rod, spoil the child" (Note: There is no verse in the Bible that says "spare the rod, spoil the child." That phrase is actually from a satirical poem called Hudibras by Samuel Butler first published in 1662.) refers to an actual physical rod (instead of a symbol of guidance and loving correction...i.e. discipleship) and that the word used for 'child' refers to a toddler or small child instead of the actual linguistic translation meaning 'young man,' then so be it.

But do you really believe that Jesus' New Covenant is for everyone *except* children? That grace, mercy, unconditional love, and forgiveness are for adults *only*?

The disciples made that mistake, and Jesus said to them,

"Let the little children come to me, and do not hinder them, for the kingdom of God belongs to such as these."
Luke 18:16

Five verses with questionable interpretations
versus following Jesus' example
...no contest.

Chapter 12

The Greatest of These is Love

"The fruit of the Spirit is love, joy, peace, patience, kindness, goodness, faithfulness, gentleness and self-control"
Galatians 5:22-23

Parenting through the fruit of the Spirit...

Love ~ Many parents say they make their parenting choices out of love, and I believe that is so very true, but if God *is* love as he says he is (and he is!), then *our* love needs to reflect *his* in every way, including in our parenting. And how does God show his love? Sacrificially, *"For God so loved the world that He gave His only Son, that whoever believes in him will not perish, but have everlasting life." (John 3:16).* Modeling God's sacrificial love in our parenting is reflected by making parenting choices based on our children's needs, not on our convenience. Responsive parenting is truly a picture of God's sacrificial, unconditional love so beautifully expressed here: *"This is how God showed his great love for us, that Christ died for us while we were still sinners" (Romans 5:8)* As we respond to our children where they are, comforting their cries, guiding their choices, providing for their needs, encouraging their individuality, we are, moment by moment, day by day, sacrificing our own convenience and desires for them.

Joy ~ Parenting can be a challenge but taking joy in the journey and in our children makes all the difference. *"Jesus, full of joy through the Holy Spirit, said, 'I praise you, Father, Lord of heaven and earth, because you have hidden these things from the wise and learned, and revealed them to little children.'"* *(Luke 10:21)* Taking time out each day to enjoy your children, or, better yet, to tell them what joy they bring to your life and specifically what unique things you enjoy about them will reconnect you with your little ones even on the most difficult of days. So, take some time to tell your children you *like* them

63

today, and list the reasons why. Then watch in wonder as they blossom before your eyes. Words of recognition and appreciation to a child are like sunshine and rain to a flower.

Peace ~ It can be so hard making parenting choices, knowing that our actions or inactions will have an incredibly profound effect on a precious little life. God knows and sees and cares about every detail of our lives and our children's lives. And, in the same way that we want our little ones to trust us with their needs and concerns and desires, God wants us to trust him and to have peace in him: *"Do not be anxious about anything, but in every situation, by prayer and petition, with thanksgiving, present your requests to God. And the peace of God, which passes understanding, will guard your hearts and your minds in Christ Jesus." (Philippians 4:6-7)* As you work through the inevitable challenges and joys and struggles and triumphs inherent in raising children, trust that God is at work in their hearts and lives, too, and that he loves your children immeasurably more than you do, as hard as that is to imagine.

Patience ~ *"Be completely humble and gentle; be patient, bearing with one another in love." (Ephesians 4:2)* Children come into our lives as small bundles with big needs who don't speak or understand our language and then proceed to grow into little people with their own temperaments, plans, and desires. Having patience and modelling that patience with our children not only helps us to guide and grow them gently, but also encourages them to exercise patience with themselves and others throughout life…a rare, but lovely gift that we can give the world through our children.

Kindness ~ My grandmother's favorite verse was *"Love is patient, love is kind. It does not envy, it does not boast, it is not proud. It does not dishonor others, it is not self-seeking, it is not easily angered, it keeps no record of wrongs." (1Corinthians 13:4-5)* This is a beautiful example of how the Bible encourages us to treat others…*including* our children. Taking time out on occasion to examine our parenting practices and evaluate them in terms of how loving and patient and kind we are to our little ones is a vital part of effective parenting. It's also important to make sure we aren't parenting 'for the neighbors.' In other words, we need to make sure that we aren't making parenting choices based on a 'who has the best kid' competition or out of embarrassment over our children's behavior. Are we easily angered by our children? Do we dredge up their mistakes time and time again? If so, consciously working to break those bad habits and replace them with love and patience and kindness will have a dramatically positive impact on our parenting.

Goodness ~ "Still other seed fell on good soil. It came up, grew and produced a crop, some multiplying thirty, some sixty, some a hundred times." (Mark 4:8) Of all things, shouldn't our very first desire in parenting our children be to till the soil of their little hearts so tenderly, so carefully, so intentionally that their hearts are "good soil," ready, eager, and willing to receive the good news of Jesus' birth, death, and resurrection? Instead of focusing on punishing our children's mistakes, thus negating the Gospel and undermining the very purpose for Jesus' suffering, shouldn't we model the grace and mercy and forgiveness we ourselves have been given?

Faithfulness ~ "I will exalt you; I will praise your name, for you have done wonderful things, plans formed of old, faithful and sure." (Isaiah 25:1) God is faithful in his promises, faithful in his love, faithful in his parenting. In all things we need to reflect his character to our children so that we share with them about God's faithfulness not only in words, but also in deeds. Faithfulness is defined as constancy, dependability, care, trustworthiness, devotion, honor, attachment, commitment.[38] So let us parents, as reflections of God, be faithful to exhibit constancy, dependability, care, trustworthiness, devotion, honor, attachment, and commitment in our parenting choices, as well.

Gentleness ~ "Let your gentleness be evident to all"...except your children. No, of course God doesn't say that. God says, *"Let your gentleness be evident to ALL"* (emphasis added) in *Philippians 4:5*. Tender, compassionate, merciful, warm-hearted, sensitive, approachable, good-humored...these are all synonyms for gentleness,[38] and gentle parenting reflects all of those qualities. And the antonyms of gentleness are...harsh, tough, violent, sharp, rigid, severe, unrelenting, unforgiving, punitive, unpleasant, pitiless, stern.[38] So let's choose gentleness in our parenting so that we let our *"gentleness be evident to all"* including (especially!) our littlest, most defenseless, and truly precious gifts from God—our children.

Self-control ~ "Like a city whose walls are broken through is a person who lacks self-control." (Proverbs 25:28) The breaking down of city walls was a tragedy of great proportions in the Bible, whereas a city gladly throwing open its gates to welcome its King was a time of rejoicing. The 'city walls' were often used metaphorically in the Bible to refer to a person's autonomy, their ability to choose right from wrong, their free will. Many times the words 'break a child's will' are thrown around and spoken as if directly from the mouth of God. But God, as our heavenly Parent, doesn't seek to *break* our will. Instead, he *invites* us to trust him and align our will with him by demonstrating his love, joy, peace, patience, kindness, goodness, faithfulness, gentleness and by his self-control in helping us in *the midst of our struggles and mistakes*. It is through building a trust-relationship with us that he gently calls us to joyfully and voluntarily align our wills out of trust and gratitude and to open our hearts and minds and lives to him, welcoming in our King. That is the heart of trust-based parenting.

"But the greatest of these is love..."
1 Corinthians 13:13b

Chapter 13

The Reality of Perception

"See that you do not look down on one of these little ones.
For I tell you that their angels in heaven always see
the face of my Father in heaven."
Matthew 18: 10

Dr. James Dobson, Michael Pearl, Tedd Tripp, Gary Ezzo, and other Christian 'child-training' parenting authors have a slew of sarcastic and disparaging names and characteristics they ascribe to children in their books and articles: *ill-tempered, wilful, bratty, defiant, self-centered, pugnacious, testy, spitfires, confirmed anarchists, obnoxious, goody two-shoes, sneaky, horrid, little revolutionaries, implacable, contentious, double trouble, Nazis, disobedient, lust-driven, slave to his desires, uncooperative, hard-headed as mules, tough-minded, unruly, irritating, pack of adolescent wolves, terrorist, twerps, confirmed revolutionary, little chameleon, negative, rebellious, sullen, stick of dynamite, flighty, spoiled brat, goof-off, fireball, snippy, difficult, prissy, groaning lump, nasty, cantankerous, rude, stubborn, sour, hostile, foolish, selfish, depraved, insane,* just to name a few.

With such a calloused and negative view of children, it really isn't surprising that the parenting tactics these child-training 'experts' promote are heavily punishment- and control-based, and even infants aren't excluded from the characterizations:

> Dr. Dobson states that some infants are *"defiant upon exit from the womb"* and *"come into the world smoking a cigar and yelling about the temperature in the delivery room."* He quips, *"A healthy baby can keep her mother or father hopping around her nursery twelve hours a day (or night) by simply forcing air past her sandpaper larynx."*[39] *(The New Strong-Willed Child)*

Tedd Tripp declares, *"Even a child in the womb and coming from the womb is wayward and sinful,"* and, *"something is wrong in the heart of the child that requires correction."[4] (Shepherding a Child's Heart)*

Such critical and unmerciful opinions of children coming from those doling out parenting advice to parents seeking Biblical guidance to help them raise their children is chilling. Here's why…

Let's face it, parents, we're human. And, as humans, we are far more likely to respond kindly to someone who we see in a positive light. No one likes to feel used or lied to or manipulated, and the words we, ourselves, use to characterize our children's behaviour [often influenced by what we've read and heard] not only reveal what our feelings are toward our children, but also strongly determine our responses to them.

Consider:

- A baby cries in the night. The parent who hears the cry as communicating a need will respond quickly and consistently. The parent who hears the cry as manipulation will likely ignore the cries.

- A toddler has a meltdown. The parent who sees a small child overwhelmed by big emotions and unable to articulate his needs will respond with empathy. The parent who sees a stubborn little dictator pitching a fit because he didn't get his own way will typically ignore or punish the toddler.

- A preschooler complains of a stomach ache every morning before being dropped off at daycare. The parent who hears a vulnerable child with limited language skills trying, in the only way she can, to express the loneliness and anxiety she feels at the daily separation will respond with understanding and comfort. The parent who hears a lie and feels manipulated will likely react with anger or impatience.

- A child comes home from school and has a meltdown when asked if he has any homework. The parent who sees a little person overwhelmed and struggling will respond with compassion and assistance. The parent who sees a lazy spoiled brat will typically react with threats and demands.

- A teenager screams, "You don't understand me!" The parent who hears the hurt and need behind the words will stop talking and start listening. The parent who hears rebellion and disrespect will likely respond with anger, punishment, or a lecture.

Parents around the world and across the ages have heard a baby's cry, coped with a toddler's meltdown, dealt with a child's anger, and faced an adolescent's attitude, and in each and every case the motivation that the parents attributed to the behavior has been the single most powerful determinant in the parents' response.

But the impact of the parents' perception is even more powerful than just a momentary appropriate or inappropriate response. The parents' perceptions all too often become the reality. In other words, who they believe they are raising is who they will raise.

Here's the thing, if you call a child a liar often enough, they will become deceptive. If you treat a child like they are manipulating you often enough, they will become conniving. If you label a child a spoiled brat, they will become impudent and rebellious.

By the same token, if you treat a child like a priceless gift, handling them with care and respect, they will grow up valuing themselves and others.

So, who are you raising, parents? An innocent child or a cunning manipulator? It's vital that you decide, because your perception of who your child is and what motivates them will influence not only your attitude toward your child, but your response to your child as well.

Remember, who you think you are raising is who you will raise! *(Whispers Through Time: Communication Through the Ages and Stages of Childhood)*

Conferring negative and critical attitudes toward children has incalculable potential to damage the parent/child relationship. And yet it is that very relationship that should reflect our trust relationship with God, including reflecting his delight in his children. God's love is unconditional, and ours should be, as well.

"Therefore be imitators of God as dear children. And walk in love, as Christ also has loved us and given Himself for us"
Ephesians 5:1-2

Chapter 14

A Person's a Person,
No Matter How Small

"Are not five sparrows sold for two pennies? And not one
of them is forgotten before God. Why, even the hairs of your
head are all numbered. Fear not; you are of more value
than many sparrows."
Luke 12:6-7

A strange dichotomy amongst the Christian child-training set is
their nearly unanimous belief that full, unadulterated personhood
begins at conception with all of the rights to protection under the
law that personhood carries versus their equally unanimous
belief that once children are born they don't deserve the status of
full personhood with all rights to protection under the law. This
conflict of interest can be seen clearly in their vehement
opposition to extending existing domestic violence laws that
protect adults to cover protection for children, as well.

Beneath the disregard for the physical protection of children
from physical punishment, though, is the deeper issue of value.
Children in these child-training manuals are spoken of as
inconveniences to be overcome, as problems to be fixed. They
are given no voice, no control over their own lives, because their
lives are not considered to be their own.

The fact is, though, that children are people. Period. And they
are people that *matter*. Their likes and dislikes *matter*. Their
interests *matter*. Their opinions *matter*. When they are externally
controlled, ordered to obey instantly and cheerfully to every
command that they are given, their personhood is disregarded
and their in-built human instinct, that God-given free will that
makes us the individuals that we were created to be, is to resist
those external controls.

In child-training manuals, though, parents are told that when a
child resists their commands, the child is being rebellious,
defiantly saying, *"I want what I want, and I want it now."* But

71

isn't that actually what the parent is saying? *"I want you to do what I want you to do, and I want you to do it now."* Instant obedience in a nutshell.

However, if you 'listen' closely to the child's behavior, which is the language of communication in childhood, you'll hear something other than *"I want what I want, and I want it now."* You'll hear…

"Why doesn't my voice count?"

"Aren't I a separate person?"

"Why don't I matter?"

"Isn't my way even worth a try?"

"Don't I count, too?"

"Is it really all about you?"

"Don't I have good ideas, too?"

"Are you always right?"

"Am I always wrong?"

"Why won't you listen?"

"Can you even hear me?"

The thing is, telling a child, or showing them through our disregard, that something they care about isn't important doesn't convince them that it doesn't matter. It just convinces them that it doesn't matter to *us*, and they often begin to feel that *they* don't matter to us, either. It is simply human nature to feel a powerful need to be heard:

> Small people have big emotions and need help processing them. Their cries as babies and shrieks and tantrums as toddlers and meltdowns as preschoolers are, literally, cries for help.

Ignoring or punishing them, or reacting with anger ourselves, simply forces them to bury their unresolved emotions and causes us to miss an opportunity to not only share our wisdom by helping them process their big feelings, but also to guide our children toward more appropriate ways to communicate as they grow. In some cases, when a child's emotions are forced underground it results in a child who simmers with hidden rage just waiting to explode again or, worse, the rage may turn inward and result in a child who is withdrawn, detached, or even depressed.

As parents, it's up to us to exercise the wisdom and maturity to control our own instinctive reaction to our children's behaviors, to find ways to work *with* them instead of against them. Having parenting tools ready and waiting for the inevitable challenges of raising little humans is wise. When emotions begin running high, and as parents we can feel our own stress levels rising, knowing we have a well-stocked parenting toolbox with tried and tested tools helps us to keep our cool so that we can parent more intentionally and effectively.

From those first tiny squeaks and mewls of a newborn, a baby's cries mature into whimpers, squeals, screams, and sobs, all communicating one thing: "I need help." When we respond to our baby's cries quickly and gently, whether it's to feed them or change them or give them a cuddle, we communicate in return, "I'm here. You can count on me."

But then there are those times when we've fed them, changed them, burped them, rocked and cuddled and walked with them, and their piercing screams still shatter the silence...and our hearts. Those are times when parents often begin to feel overwhelmed, stressed, sometimes even resentful and angry because no matter what they try, they can't 'fix' their baby and make them stop crying. It is in those moments of frustration and distress that we need to breathe in deeply to calm ourselves, then stop stressing over trying to 'fix' our baby and instead whisper in our little one's ear, "I'm

here. I've got you. We'll get through this together."
They may not understand our words, but they will hear
our heart.

Once a baby reaches the crawling, exploring,
discovering stage, they often have a great time
experimenting with the volume, pitch, and range of
their voice, much to the chagrin of their parents and
pretty much everyone else within earshot. The ear-
shattering squeals and bellows and joyful shrieks at this
stage can be disconcerting to us parents, to say the
least, especially when our little falsetto performs their
operatic interpretation in public places such as doctor's
offices, libraries, and restaurants.

This is a prime opportunity to exercise the power of the
whisper. If a picture is worth a thousand words, then a
whisper is worth two thousand when it comes to
parenting. In the same way that the instinctive human
reaction to someone raising their voice is to raise our
voice one octave higher, to out-shout the shouter, to
over-power the person powering-up on us, the
instinctive human response to someone whispering is to
quiet down, to lean-in, to listen.

When the first shriek splits the silence, try holding a
finger to your lips, smile like you're inviting them to
join in on a secret, and whisper, "It's whisper time.
Let's use our little voices together." Making a game out
of it invites cooperation rather than demands obedience,
a much more effective parenting technique, and
practicing little voices together demonstrates what you
want your little one to do instead of simply telling them
what you don't want them to do.

Don't be surprised if it takes many repetitions over
several outings before your little one begins to get the
idea, though. As with all parenting, time and patience
and an awareness (and acceptance!) of what is normal
for each developmental stage is key.

Toddlers and preschoolers are famous for their big tantrums sparked by big emotions and big frustrations. Obviously being aware of and avoiding tantrum triggers such as hunger, tiredness, and over-stimulation is important. But even with the most proactive parenting, there may still be times when our little ones have unexpected, incomprehensible, inconsolable tantrums.

When faced with a toddler or preschooler in the throes of a tantrum, if we know what caused the tantrum, you can validate the emotion with a soft-voiced, "You're angry (disappointed, sad, hurt) because you (fill in the blank)." Often just hearing their feelings put into words is enough to calm a toddler who is frustrated at their inability to express themselves, but sometimes they need a bit of time and support to work through their big emotions.

If the tantrum continues, stay calm and present and remember that you are modeling self-control and self-regulation when you practice those skills instead of having an adult-style tantrum in response to your child's tantrum. Instead of trying to control your child's outburst with demands or threats or bribes, you can simply stay close and whisper, "I hear you. I'm here."

The secret of the whisper in taming a tantrum can be seen in the difference between dumping a bucket of water on a fire, which can force the fire underground where it may smolder and reignite unexpectedly, versus spraying a gentle mist on the fire so it's slowly and fully extinguished, leaving the ground saturated so the fire won't reignite. Settling your little one quietly and patiently with a whisper is the gentle mist that saturates them with your unconditional love and support so they don't simmer with hidden rage that may erupt spontaneously again.

No matter the problem, kindness is always the right response. When your child is having a problem, stop, listen, then respond to the need, not the behavior. The behavior can be addressed later, after the need has been met, because only then is the door to effective communication truly open.

The thing to keep in mind is that there is no cure for childhood. There is no parenting secret that will 'work' to keep children from being children. Children will cry. They will tantrum. They will yell and giggle and climb and run and throw things and build things and hit and hug and explore and make glorious mistakes and incredible discoveries. They will be human. They will be children. And that's more than okay. That's beautiful, messy, wonderful childhood, just as it should be.

Parents are guides through the incredible journey of childhood, not to keep their children from experiencing childhood, but to keep them safe as they learn the magnificent life lessons that childhood has to offer. (*Whispers Through Time: Communication Through the Ages and Stages of Childhood*)

The title of this chapter, "A person's a person, no matter how small" is from Dr. Seuss' children's book *Horton Hears a Who!* in which a gentle elephant is the only one who can hear the voice of a Who, a small person from Whoville. The entire civilization of Who's are endangered because no one but Horton will listen to the voice of such a small person. As Horton tries to save the Who's, he tells them…

"Don't give up! I believe in you all!
A person's a person, no matter how small!

The mayor of Whoville responds by urging the Who's to join their voices together and make themselves heard…

"We've GOT to make noises in greater amounts!
So, open your mouth, lad! For every voice counts!"

And that is what children naturally do when they feel unheard. They *"make noises,"* via that language of communication in childhood, their behavior, with greater and greater amounts of persistent, insistent resistance.

There is a solution, though. We can work *with* our little people instead of against them. We can connect with them by caring about the little things that matter to little people. We can communicate with them by being the first to listen instead of insisting on being the first to be heard. And we can cooperate with them by finding ways to make sure that everyone's likes and dislikes and plans and ideas and opinions are taken into account so that, *"Every voice counts."*

> *"I cried out to the Lord with my voice,*
> *and he heard me from his Holy mountain"*
> *Psalm 3:4*

Chapter 15

Stealing God's Gift:
Free Will is a Gift to be Nurtured,
Not a Curse to be Broken

"Let us then approach God's throne of grace with
confidence, so that we may receive mercy and find grace to
help us in our time of need."
Hebrews 4:16

> *"Many parents in using the rod of correction on their*
> *child do so with an obvious lack of vigor and often stop*
> *short of the child's will being completely broken ...*
> *Both my wife and I have often remarked that it is good*
> *that one of our children was not our firstborn. This*
> *particular child who came along later in our family*
> *was extremely willful and rebellious toward our*
> *authority and would often require sessions of*
> *correction lasting from one to two hours in length*
> *before the will would finally be broken ... Even though*
> *you may think these methods of correction that God has*
> *ordered parents to carry out are bestial, abusive, and*
> *unloving, you are the one who is bestial, abusive, and*
> *unloving if you don't obey God in this matter.*
> *Moreover, if you do not obey God your child likely will*
> *not be saved unless the Lord supernaturally in His*
> *mercy does so despite your disobedience."[6] (Ronald E.*
> *Williams, The Correction and Salvation of Children)*

> *"She then administers about ten slow, patient licks on*
> *his bare legs. He cries in pain. If he continues to show*
> *defiance by jerking around and defending himself, or*
> *by expressing anger, then she will wait a moment and*

again lecture him and again spank him. When it is
obvious he is totally broken, she will hand him the rag
and very calmly say, "Johnny, clean up your mess." He
should very contritely wipe up the water [about
spanking a 3-year-old]" (Pearl, p. 62) ... "Never
reward delayed obedience by reversing the sentence.
And, unless all else fails, don't drag him to the place of
cleansing. Part of his training is to come submissively.
However, if you are just beginning to institute training
on an already rebellious child, who runs from
discipline and is too incoherent to listen, then use
whatever force is necessary to bring him to bay. If you
have to sit on him to spank him then do not hesitate.
And hold him there until he is surrendered. Prove that
you are bigger, tougher, more patiently enduring and
are unmoved by his wailing. Defeat him totally. Accept
no conditions for surrender. No compromise. You are
to rule over him as a benevolent sovereign. Your word
is final (p. 49)"[17] (Michael Pearl, To Train Up a Child)

Where, exactly, did the pseudo-Biblical idea that a parent must
break a child's will originate? How did a person's God-given
will, their freedom of choice, their strength and individuality,
come to be seen as the root of all sin that must be purged? At
what point did "defeating" a child so that they are "totally
broken" become the goal of Christian parenting?

Let's go back to the model of servant leadership set by Jesus
who said, *"I stand at the door and knock..." (Revelations 3:20)*
Knock what? Knock humans on their backsides and pin them
down while pummelling them until they are utterly defeated?
Knock small children around until they are totally broken?

No, of course not. Jesus says, *"I stand at the door and knock. If*
anyone hears my voice and opens the door, I will come in and
eat with that person, and they with me." Jesus doesn't barge in
making demands to prove how big and tough he is. Jesus invites
us to open the door of our lives and to invite him in as an
honored guest, in return.

Look also at *Deuteronomy 30:19* where God shares that it is
from him that our ability to choose originates, *"I have set before*

you life and death, blessing and curse; therefore choose life, that you and your descendants may live." Note that God doesn't *demand* that we submit our free, God-given will, our ability to choose, to him. He simply *invites* us to align our will with his.

And look at *James 4:8, "Draw near to God and He will draw near to you."* God doesn't chase us down, "sit on" us, or "use whatever force is necessary" (see Pearl quote above) to strong-arm us into submission. He reaches out to us and inspires us and opens his arms to us, inviting us into the safety and comfort and wholeness of a relationship with Love Himself.

Our will is a *gift*, an opportunity to *choose* right from wrong, and the vehicle through which God calls us to choose his Son. Without this amazing and wonderful gift, without the freedom to use our free will, Jesus' suffering and death on the Cross would be pointless.

Sin is a moot point in light of the grace we've been given. Grace is the point. The *whole* point. Everything leading up to the Cross pointed to the Cross, everything was settled on the Cross, and on the Cross in the outstretched arms of Jesus grace was born. Sin only matters in the sense that when we voluntarily choose to stay within the boundaries God has given us, we are closer to him, more in-tune with him, and more aligned with his will. He does not stray from us, not ever. But we do stray from him. We are human, and as humans we learn by doing, by experiencing, by exercising our free will as we stretch and grow and discover and make mistakes and overcome life and are overcome by life, each trial and failure and success a learning experience. God doesn't chase us down and crash through the walls we've put up and drag us back to repentance. He waits for us, always available, always forgiving, always loving us unconditionally, but never giving up as he calls out to us, inviting us gently to himself.

When it comes to parenting, we all know that some of God's children are created with a remarkable strength of will, a powerful drive to explore and discover, an insatiable thirst for knowledge, an incredible need to know and be known, and with more energy than can be contained in a small body. Their frequent challenges to 'the way things are' can feel overwhelming to the most patient of parents, and their sometimes epic meltdowns when all of that extreme energy explodes out of their small frames can act like a tidal wave of emotion that gets everyone swept up in the maelstrom. These children who are given the gift of an indomitable spirit have all of the amazing characteristics of future world leaders, but their gifts need to be grown and nurtured and developed, not contained, stunted, and crushed.

A popular child-training book by Dr. James Dobson, *The New Strong-Willed Child,* has a markedly different approach to parenting strong-willed children, however: *"Some strong-willed children absolutely demand to be spanked, and their wishes should be granted. . . two or three stinging strokes on the legs or buttocks with a switch are usually sufficient to emphasize the point, 'You must obey me.'"*[39] In addition to the disputable Biblical interpretations of the 'rod' verses and the misuse of the word 'obey' in translating from the original language of the Bible, there is a fundamental difference in philosophies revealed here. In the positive parenting approach, children are born perfect and need only to be guided through the normal stages and behaviors of childhood. In the punitive parenting approach, children are born sinful and must be forced to submit to superior authority.

On a purely logical level, why would we fight a child for control when what we really want is for them to be in control of themselves? Why not, instead, help them to process those big emotions and learn how to direct their own energy and develop their own ability to control themselves? Why not follow Jesus' example and invite our strong little future leaders to walk alongside us in tandem to learn and grow and discover together for the oh-so-brief season of their childhood?

On a practical level, though, the question is, "How can we partner with our children in positive and peaceful ways to guide them gently and effectively?"

Here is a chapter from *The Gentle Parent: Positive, Practical, Effective Discipline* to get you started on your gentle journey with your own little future leaders:

'The Gift of a Strong-Willed Child'

There are some children who are born into the world with the incredible life-gift of a strong will and an indomitable spirit. These children are often deeply misunderstood, and there are rows of books lining bookstore shelves with instructions about how to break their will, how to subdue their spirit, how to force their obedience. What an incredible loss of leadership, passion, and insight this world suffers when parents follow these punitive parenting practices. Not only can we parent these gifted children with gentleness and respect, but the gifts we get in return are priceless!

Take a look at some of the common descriptions used when referring to the characteristics of a strong-willed child:

Demanding, Insistent, Stubborn, Bossy, Cocky, Difficult, Challenging, Fixated, Contrary, Rebellious, Defiant

Now look at some of the common characteristics of adults who are world leaders, CEO's, entrepreneurs, innovators, world-class athletes, and the like:

Decisive, Determined, Persistent, Authoritative, Confident, Valiant, Gutsy, Committed, Resourceful, Nonconforming, Bold

Note that the characteristics are the same, but the characterizations are negative when applied to a child and positive when applied to an adult.

Other characteristics of strong-willed children that coincide with the characteristics of adult leaders in their fields are:

- They are typically highly creative and intelligent.

- They are usually passionate and intense in their interests and beliefs.

- They often have an insatiable need to know 'why.'

- They typically learn by doing.

- They tend to have an intense need to test the status quo.

- They are typically highly perfection-oriented, but often that is focused on their expectations of themselves instead of others.

- They tend to need high levels of validation.

- They usually have an intense need to be heard.

- They often have a strong need for emotional safety.

- They tend to be resistant to change unless they feel like they have some control over the change.

- They are often highly sensitive.

- They are typically intensely focused on their latest project or interest.

- They tend to be conscientious and highly committed.

- They are usually intensely independent.

While there's no doubt that it's a challenge having a child who seems to challenge everything, there are ways to work with them rather than against them to preserve and nurture their unique gifts. Maintaining a healthy parent/child relationship is vital as you work to find a balance between setting limits with your richly spirited child while not limiting their freedom to stretch and grow and develop into the person they were created to be.

The key to preserving your trust relationship with your child is remaining calm and present and supportive, even while setting and maintaining reasonable boundaries. It is helpful to remember that the most strong-willed children tend to be the ones who identify the most strongly with their parents. So instead of viewing their seemingly constant challenges as defiance or attempts to thwart authority, work to parent from a place of understanding that your strong-willed child is actually on a discovery mission and is doing endless 'research' on you by testing and retesting and digging and chiseling to discover all of your quirks and foibles and ups and downs and strengths and weaknesses. This kind of testing isn't negative unless you make it into a battle of wills instead of responding with gentle, respectful guidance. Taking this stance will help you to keep from seeing the challenges as personal insults and, instead, see the challenges as attempts to learn and grow and understand.

There is no doubt, though, that parenting a child with the gift of a strong will is a constant exercise in patience and self-regulation. The personal growth you will experience is invaluable as you seek to parent with empathy and wisdom and compassion, but it can be draining and will often stretch you far, far out of your comfort zone. Knowing that and being prepared for it will help you cope with the inevitable stresses, and being ready ahead of time with some specific strategies for handling the challenges will help you to respond calmly and effectively.

This is a good place to revisit the Three C's of gentle discipline—Connection, Communication, and Cooperation.

Connection ~ Maintaining a secure connection with your spirited child is vital. It is the springboard from which all of your interactions with your child will originate, and it is the touchstone to which you will both return, again and again and again, when your relationship gets strained and stained and stretched.

- Play word games, board games, rough-and-tumble outdoor games, silly face in the mirror games. Play is the language of childhood, so make sure to speak your child's language every day.

- Laugh together. Humor is an undervalued parenting tool. But it lowers defenses, inspires smiles, brings people together, and reconnects hearts.

- Read storybooks, chapter books, travel brochures, encyclopedias, anything that will inspire you to dream together, talk, plan, get excited, share interests.

- Focus more on who your child is than on what your child does. Remember, you're growing a person, not fixing a problem. So make sure to spend time getting to know the person, not just the child. It doesn't have to cost anything. Just walk together, talk together, share ice cream cones, spot shapes in the clouds, and enjoy each other.

Communication ~ Children have their own 'inner world' of thoughts and plans and problems and worries and hopes and dreams that are occupying their time and attention, so a lack of cooperation is often simply the result of having a different agenda than we do. Getting some insight into that 'inner world' is key in guiding and growing them respectfully.

- Listen with your heart. Listen 'between the lines' to what your child is communicating through their behavior. Listen and listen and listen some more. That is always, always the first step in communicating with your child.

- Reflect, connect, and redirect. Reflect what you hear, whether it's communicated by your child's behavior or their words. This not only validates their emotions and lets them know that you hear and understand them, but it also helps them to understand their own emotions. For instance, if your child is upset that he can't have a cookie after brushing his teeth for bedtime, try saying, "I hear you. You're upset because you want a cookie." Then reestablish your connection, "I like cookies, too!" and offer a solution, "How about we go pick out the two best cookies and put them in a special container that we can take to the park in the morning?"

- Don't take non-compliance as a personal insult. A strong-willed child is very much their own person with their own agenda. Focus on inviting cooperation instead of demanding obedience. Whether it's staying in bed or cleaning up or whatever the issue, make it a team effort and come up with a game plan ahead of time. For example, you could say, "You seem to be having trouble staying in bed at night. What do you think would help you to be more ready to go to sleep when it's time for bed?" or "It's important to pick up our things so they don't get broken, let's put on the timer and work together for ten minutes and see who gets the most picked up."

- Make a firm commitment not to resort to punishments to control behavior. The resentment that comes from being punished absolves children in their own minds of responsibility. It doesn't teach them responsibility, and resentment can actually cause a lot of the behaviors you are trying to avoid.

- Communicate daily, outwardly to your child and inwardly to yourself, the positive aspects of your child's personality. When the focus is on 'fixing' a child, they get the message that they are somehow broken, and that is not a healthy self-image to take into adulthood.

- 'No' is not a complete thought. It is an imperative, a command. It doesn't teach. It tells. If you want your child to learn to think like an adult, take the time to explain your adult thinking.

- Remember that children, especially when they are upset, open 'conversations' through their behavior, and it's up to us, the only adults in the relationship, to gently guide them toward continuing those conversations verbally as well as equipping them with the resources to be able to do so.

- Also keep in mind that the social mores of rudeness simply aren't inborn and don't apply to early interactions with our children. They are learned by imitating how we as parents behave. Politeness is a heart issue that cannot be imposed by the will of another unless we want it to only be an external façade instead of a heartfelt courtesy. Helping your strong-willed child learn to speak kindly means speaking kindly to your child as well as offering guidance when they've been rude such as saying, "That is not a nice tone of voice" or "That isn't a kind thing to say" and then offering a do-over "Can you try saying that to me again more nicely? I'll always try my best to be nice to you, and I would like you to try to do the same for me." (see Appendix B for more ideas)

Cooperation ~ Always keep at the forefront of your parenting goals that you are seeking thoughtful cooperation, not mindless compliance. That way you will remember to treat your child as a thoughtful individual with ideas and needs and feelings of their own instead of a mindless drone there to do your bidding.

- Set clear limits and explain them in age-appropriate terms. Remember, if you want to invite cooperation, you have to actually issue the invitation to cooperate!

- Limit the number of limits. Spirited children are often stressed children simply because of their own intense emotions and reactions to things, so set them up for success by keeping your limits few and clear and by maintaining them consistently.

- Make sure to let your child have a voice in determining the limits so they feel like they have some control over their lives and so they feel some ownership over the limits.

- Brainstorm together ways of helping everyone to work together. Some ideas are to come up with hand signals or words that remain your little secret codes to indicate when it's time to leave the park or to do homework or to dial the activity level or noise volume down a few notches.

- Invite cooperation by creating daily routines together. Don't be surprised if your child ends up being the one who is a stickler for following the routine, even to the point of nagging *you* to follow it. These gifted children tend to be all-in, fully focused and committed, and they'll expect you to be the same!

- Cooperate with your child's needs and personality by working with them rather than against them. For instance, if you know that your child has a hard time leaving a project, give them plenty of time to find a good stopping point when you need them to leave it for a while. Or if you know that your child has a hard time following directions at bedtime, try writing or drawing the tasks that need to be done (i.e. toothbrushing, pajamas, etc.) on ping-pong balls and put them in a small 'bedtime jar' so your child can feel some control over their routine as they independently pick out the balls one by one for a 'surprise' nighttime order of tasks or take them all out and decide what order to do them in themselves.

- If you are already locked in a head-to-head power struggle, put away your boxing gloves so your child will (eventually!) feel safe putting away theirs. When you battle with your child, you may win a skirmish or two, but you will lose the treasure…your trust relationship. Putting away the gloves means slowing down, breathing through your own emotions, and finding a way to work through the issue together. Remember, you're the adult in the relationship, but that doesn't give you the right to overpower your child; it gives you the responsibility to empower your child. That involves modeling the tools of diplomacy— communication, cooperation, compromise—that you want your child to stock in their own emotional toolkit.

Remember, the children who come into the world with their 'boxing gloves on' so to speak are often the ones who become the biggest world changers. It's not easy raising these little world-changers, I know (*Believe me, I know. Two of my six are world-changers-in-the-making!*), but the rewards are phenomenal!

"The Lord's loving-kindnesses indeed never cease,
for his compassions never fail."
Lamentations 3:22

Chapter 16

Listening is Where Love Begins

*"Because he bends down to listen, I will pray
as long as I have breath."*
Psalm 116:2

Children communicate with their whole beings. They speak with words, with actions, with emotions, with expressions. They are the greatest of communicators because they hold nothing back, and when they feel unheard they will keep trying and trying in increasing volume and action to break through. But, as the frustration of not feeling heard mounts, their ability to articulate decreases rapidly because their executive brain is being flooded with stress hormones, shutting down the language and logic center of the brain and sending them spiraling into the instinctual, impulse driven portion of their brain. (see Chapter Eight) But they don't stop trying to be heard. They simply begin speaking almost entirely through their behavior, often in very negative ways, and we suddenly find ourselves in the midst of a behavior challenge.

The thing is, though, that most behavior challenges can be avoided if we simply start out by listening. We are the only adults in the relationship, and it is up to *us* to exercise patience, to slow down and get down and give our little ones our time and attention and really hear them. It can be challenging at times, for sure, to understand what our children are trying to say, *really* say, when their words and actions can seem so unreasonable to the adult mind. But if we listen with our hearts, our eyes, our ears, all of our senses, we will see and hear and understand. Frustrations will fade. Conflicts will cease. Hearts will heal. And the connection that leads to cooperation will be established, with communication as the vehicle. Connection, Communication, Cooperation…the heart of gentle parenting.

It is through our intentional connection with our children that the door to communication is opened and the path to cooperation is paved. The door to communication, of course, swings both ways, which means that by consciously listening to our children we are not only really hearing them and preventing behavior issues from escalating, or avoiding them entirely, but we are also effectively creating the avenue through which we will be heard, as well:

> Often the first question parents ask when seeking parenting guidance is, "How can I get my child to listen?" There's a wealth of frustration in those words that parents everywhere can understand and empathize with, but there are deeper questions that need to be asked before that one can be answered. The first question is *"How, exactly, do you as a parent define listening?"* The second is *"What do you believe is the purpose of listening?"* Finally, and perhaps most importantly, *"How well do you, yourself, listen?"*

> Take a moment before continuing to read and think about your definition of listening. Keep that definition, the one you've been operating from as a parent, in mind as you read on:

> Listening is defined as *to pay attention to, to take notice of, to receive.*

> Colloquially, though, and certainly in parenting, the word listening is often used to mean *to heed, to acknowledge, to obey.* Those meanings, however, are actually responses to listening rather than listening itself. What parents are typically asking when they say, *"How can I get my child to listen?"* is *"How can I get my child to* obey?"

> Now think about times in your life when you didn't feel heard, whether it was in your own childhood, or in an adult relationship, your work environment, or another area of your life. How did that make you feel? Did you feel hurt? Unimportant? Dismissed? Misunderstood? Ignored? Examine those feelings and see if they bear any similarity to how you feel when your child doesn't appear to be listening to you. Ask yourself what that

says about your need to be heard by your child. Is it obedience you're seeking or something deeper? Could your strong reaction to your child not listening to you be evidence of your own unmet needs or hurts from your past or present relationships?

Often the key to communication problems in parent/child relationships lies in the parent first working toward resolving their own hurts and finding ways of meeting their own needs. Once the parent has reached a place of peace in their own heart, they are able to focus on bringing that peace to their parenting. Listening can then become a mutual interaction, a means of communication and connection instead of being a source of conflict and a trigger for a negative parental emotional reaction.

Finally, take a moment and honestly ask yourself how well you, yourself, listen to your child. Remember, children learn best by imitation. What are you teaching them by your own example? Do you maintain eye contact with your child when they tell you their endless stories about lizards or superheroes or rocks? Do you let them explain why they need four bandages for an invisible scrape or why they can't possibly go to bed wearing purple pajamas? Do you give them your full attention when they speak, or are your thoughts occupied with what you want to say next or how you're going to make them obey? Do you insist that they listen to you first, that they hear and understand your point of view, before you're willing to listen to their viewpoint or explanation or problem?

For effective communication to take place, both parties need to hear the other. If both are focused on trying to be heard at the same time, neither will end up being heard. As the only adult in the parent/child relationship, it's up to you to listen first, to understand first, to acknowledge and validate your child first. You have the maturity and self-control to be patient and wait to be heard. Your child doesn't, especially when emotions are running high.

The reality is that parents who don't really listen to their children tend to have children who really don't listen to their parents. The flipside is that children whose parents listen to them, children who feel heard, tend to listen better to their parents.

That's not the end of it, though. Once parents have resolved their own issues with needing to feel heard and are working on modeling good listening to their children, there's the issue of the children's own immature listening skills to address. The modeling of those skills by parents in and of itself is a powerful teacher, but parents can facilitate their children's learning by identifying specific areas their children seem to have the most trouble with when it comes to listening and communication.

There are three components of verbal communication: listening, processing, and responding.

Listening is the first step in effective communication. If there is a problem at this level, it may be that your child doesn't feel heard or it may be an attention issue or a language issue. Listening, as mentioned earlier, is defined as *to pay attention to, to take notice of, to receive*...all meanings that also apply to the idea of connection. Solutions to these issues are, therefore, connection-based. Working on being in-tune with your child will help you to discern whether they don't feel heard, in which case you can intentionally reconnect with them and focus on actively listening to them, or if you need to eliminate distractions when communicating with them so they can more easily focus their attention on you, or if you need to work on finding more age-appropriate language to express yourself.

Processing is the next step in effective communication. Problems at this level can be difficult to discern because they are internal to the child as the child attempts to interpret what's been said and decide on an appropriate response. If your child seems to be attentively listening in the first step in communication, but struggles and gets stuck in the processing step, it can simply be a sign that you need to back up and try a different approach in the listening step and help them to receive the message you're trying to convey. Rarely, though, it can be a sign of a processing disorder such as attention-deficit disorder, auditory processing disorder, or other processing issues that may need to be evaluated.

> *Note: If you have any concerns about your child's communication skills or believe there may be a communication delay, having a professional evaluation sooner rather than later is a good idea. Discovering any issues, learning how to accommodate your child's communication needs, and starting appropriate early interventions can make a world of difference for your child and your relationship.*

The last step in effective communication is responding. It is here that parents' true issues with their child's listening tend to reveal themselves. Parents who want their child to comply with requests or obey commands without question or delay will, themselves, have the most issues with this step.

Ideally, a child's response in most situations should be considered and thoughtful. A child needs to feel free to ask for explanations so that they can learn about their parents' thought processes. A child who feels confident enough to respond with questions and even alternative suggestions opens the communication channel to an exchange of ideas, desires, and needs on both sides and leads to a more cooperative parent/child relationship.

Parents who are focused on control often find the idea of an interactive response rather than instant, unquestioning obedience from their child to be an uncomfortable concept. It's in that exchange of thoughts, though, that children learn how an adult thinks and that they begin to internalize the belief systems and values parents ultimately want their children to take into adulthood.

Identifying where the breakdown in communication with your child occurs, whether it's in your own visceral response because of unmet needs, or it's in the listening step, the processing step, or the responding step, will help you to make whatever changes are necessary. Don't feel that you have to minutely analyze every interaction or conversation with your child, but instead pay attention to the overall atmosphere of communication in your relationship and be ready to step in and make adjustments as needed.

As your child grows and their grasp of language expands, your communication approach will need to evolve to meet their changing needs and abilities. The one thing that won't ever change, though, is the need to listen, really *listen* to your child.

I love the quote, *"Listening is where love begins,"* from Fred Rogers, best known for his PBS television show, *Mister Rogers' Neighborhood,* but I would add that, in parenting as in all relationships in life, *'Listening is where listening begins.'* (*Whispers Through Time: Communication Through the Ages and Stages of Childhood*)

"Wisdom from above is first pure, then peaceable, gentle, open to reason, full of mercy and good fruits, impartial and sincere."
James 3:17

Chapter 17

Even Complaining is Communication

*"Morning, noon, and night I complain and groan,
and he listens to my voice."
Psalm 55:17*

One of the single most annoying stages children go through is
the whining and complaining stage. All children complain at one
time or another, but that incessant, high-pitched whine and the
accompanying complaints that seem to characterize the
preschool and early childhood crowd can make us want to run
and hide in a closet or act like a child ourselves and stick our
fingers in our ears and hum really loudly to drown it out.

But, let's face it, parents, we complain and whine and moan and
groan, too. In fact, often what we're complaining and whining
and moaning and groaning about is our children complaining
and whining and moaning and groaning! It's simply human
nature to need to communicate when we are upset or stressed or
overwhelmed or just plain out-of-sorts.

And what do we need when we complain? Correction or
commiseration? When we complain about our children not
listening, do we want our friends to tell us to stop being
ungrateful and start counting our blessings or do we simply need
an, "I hear you. I've been there," from a fellow parent? When
we come home from a long day at work and complain about the
boss passing us over for a promotion do we want, "Just be glad
you have a job," or do we just need to hear, "That is unfair. I'm
so sorry that happened," from a loving partner? When we
complain about missing an important appointment because we
were running late, do we want to be lectured about the value of
punctuality or do we just need an, "That's too bad. I've had that
happen to me, too" from a good friend?

What we really want when we complain is simply to be heard, to
be comforted, to know we aren't alone. We don't necessarily

want or need advice, but we do need support. We don't need to be rescued from our problems, though sometimes a helping hand is appreciated, but we do need to be supported as we work through them. And our children have those same human needs:

It's seven o'clock and you're finishing up the dishes before starting bedtime baths. And then it starts…the whining. Every. Single. Night. Your four-year-old knows the routine. She knows you are going to read her favorite bedtime book. She knows you will let her choose which pajamas to wear. She knows she has to brush her teeth. But that doesn't stop her from standing in the kitchen night after night whining about the same things.

So what's the deal? Short-term memory loss? An innate desire to drive you crazy? A disorder of the vocal cords that makes using a normal voice impossible after the sun sets and every time she doesn't get her way *all day long*?!?

Here's a shocker for you: Whining is actually a sign of maturity! Yep, that unnerving, endless, nails-on-a-chalkboard, make-your-head-explode whine is a sign that your little one is growing up and, get this, gaining self-control! I can see your heads shaking, but read on, parents, caregivers, and bleeding ears of the world, read on.

Whining, believe it or not, is an advanced skill. Babies come into the world with exactly one form of verbal communication--crying. They may smack their lips and root for the breast when hungry. They may arch their back or wiggle in discomfort when they need a diaper change. But when physical expressions don't result in needs being met or their needs are emotional rather than physical, then crying is always the 'default' communication. Every need, every discomfort, every bit of loneliness or anxiety or frustration or stress has to be communicated through that one single venue.

Over time as babies grow into toddlers, they begin to learn new ways to communicate, pointing, grunting, picking up a few words here and there, and they move into a more interactive stage wherein they make attempts to communicate in these new ways, but fall back very quickly into crying if they aren't understood and responded to quickly.

As time goes on, toddlerhood gives way to the preschool years and language skills advance, becoming the main source of communication for a little one. But even so, their grasp of language is limited and their prefrontal cortexes (center of forethought/pre-thinking skills) are still developing. This leads to a rather dichotomous situation in which they know what they want to say, but often can't quite put the words together quickly or clearly enough for us oh-so-impatient adults.

As they work to communicate, their frustration levels rise and stress hormones sap the blood flow from those underdeveloped 'thinking' portions of their brains and, just when they need the use of language the most, they begin to lose the ability to articulate their needs. As toddlers they would fall quickly back into crying at this point, but as preschoolers their more advanced self-control helps them to avoid immediately dissolving into tears and, instead, they fall into the 'middle-ground' of whining.

Whining is, in fact, just an advanced form of crying and, as such, is just as grating on the nerves as crying because it is designed to get the attention of a caregiver. The difference is actually in our attitudes toward whining. We accept crying as a normal part of baby and toddlerhood, but label the whining of a preschooler 'bratty' and 'spoiled' and refuse to listen to them until they 'use their normal voice' just when they need us to listen the most!

If we, as adults, would adjust our mindsets to accept the normalcy of whining, it would lose a bit of its power to annoy while enabling us to respond empathetically to our children when they're mustering all their newly-developed coping skills to avoid a meltdown.

So, what can we do when our little ones lapse into 'whine-eze' and we feel like tearing our hair out? Well, as always, an ounce of prevention is worth a pound of cure:

- Pay attention to the time of day whining seems to occur most often.

- Watch for triggers such as hunger, missed naps, and over-hurried schedules.

- Make whatever adjustments you can to prevent the whining before it starts.

- If all else fails and the whining does commence, remember that your little one is struggling to communicate in that moment. Respond by slowing down, sitting with them or kneeling down in front of them, and giving them your full attention.

- Use a quiet, soothing tone to reassure them, and listen patiently all the way through as they work their way back through the frustration and find the words to express themselves.

- You may not be able to give them the toy or snack or whatever else it is they want at that moment, but giving them the chance to be heard is often enough to forestall an all-out meltdown.

More than anything, though, giving your little ones the gift of your time and attention when they need it most (and often seem to deserve it least) will help foster that all-important connection that provides the basis for gentle guidance and boundary-setting. And, as an added bonus, children who feel heard tend to outgrow the whining stage much earlier than children who feel like they have to fight to be heard. (*Whispers Through Time: Communication Through the Ages and Stages of Childhood*)

> *"Then you shall call, and the LORD will answer; you shall cry, and he will say, 'Here I am.'"*
> *Isaiah 58:9*

Chapter 18

The Trouble with Kids Today

*"I do not set aside the grace of God for if righteousness could be
gained through the law, then Christ
died for nothing!"
Galatians 2:21*

Where did the concept originate that we should, or even that we
could, punish our children into perfection when God says
perfection isn't possible? We're human. We're imperfect. With
Jesus as the measuring stick, we will always come up short.
Luckily for us, we have a Father who loves us just as we are
instead of measuring us to see what we aren't.

Isn't it unbelief, in and of itself, though, to decide that God was
wrong when he declared that Jesus was and is the only perfect
human? (Hebrews 4:15) And aren't we emptying the Cross of its
power and its message when we insist that our children must
bear the consequences of their mistakes? *We've* been freed from
the consequences of *our* mistakes. Don't we want our children to
have the same experience, the same *freely offered* gift?

Yes, in the world there are laws and consequences for breaking
those laws. There are jobs that can be lost, appointments that
may be missed, and relationships that can suffer. But do we want
to reflect the world or do we want to reflect the hard-won grace
and mercy of the Cross to our children? Do we want to be our
children's first taste of the richness and beauty and depth of love
and forgiveness of a perfect Father or do we want to be their first
taste of the harshness of a fallen world?

God offers grace to all, *including* our children. Grace is even
offered to unregenerate sinners as God's arms remain open and
his voice calls them to him even to that moment before death
steals their last breath. After the moment passes and death
descends, though, the die has been cast, the choice made, and the
choice determines the direction. Even then, the human choice

remains, as, against God's deepest desires for his children, their free will delivers them to their choice of destinations. But until that last breath, God's door is ALWAYS open. His invitation is ALWAYS available. And the choice is ALWAYS ours to accept grace or to turn from it.

If grace is offered freely even to the unregenerate, how could it not be offered to our children? And if grace is offered freely to our children, how will they know if we don't show them?

And yet, our human minds cannot help but ask, isn't punishment necessary to parent effectively? Isn't a lack of effective parenting the trouble with kids today?

Consider...

> Effective parenting and, more specifically, effective discipline, doesn't require punishment. Equating discipline with punishment is an unfortunate, but common misconception. The root word in discipline is actually *disciple* which in the verb form means to guide, lead, teach, model, and encourage. In the noun form *disciple* means one who embraces the teaching of, follows the example of, and models their life after.
>
> On the flip side, the root word in punishment is the Latin word *punire* which in verb form means to penalize, chastise, castigate, inflict harm, humiliate.[40] There is no noun form of *punire* or its English equivalent, punishment.
>
> Many of today's most popular self-proclaimed parenting 'experts' equate physical punishment with discipline and go to great lengths to describe the best methods and tools for hitting children as well as instructing parents to maintain a calm, controlled, and even cheerful demeanor as they 'lovingly' hit their children.
>
> It is interesting to note here that, when it comes to the law, crimes of passion are treated as less heinous than premeditated, planned, and purposefully executed

crimes which are termed 'in cold blood.' And yet when physically punishing a child, a crime in many places across the globe, hitting in anger or frustration (i.e. passion) is deemed wrong by proponents of spanking, while hitting children with calm and deliberate intent (i.e. premeditation) is encouraged.

It is also interesting to note that, in the not-too-distant past, husbands hitting their wives was also viewed as not only a societal norm, but also a necessary part of maintaining a harmonious, successful marriage. In fact, a man who epitomizes the words calm and controlled, Sean Connery, shared his thoughts on the 'reasonable smacking' of his wife in a 1987 interview with Barbara Walters in which he explained the necessity of using punitive methods to control women.

The core belief behind 'reasonable smacking' of wives was that there was no other effective way to control them. I agree. If controlling another human being is the goal, then force is necessary. Fear, intimidation, threats, power-plays, physical pain, those are the means of control.

But, if growing healthy humans is the goal, then building trust relationships, encouraging, guiding, leading, teaching, and communicating are the tools for success.

Many parents simply don't know what else to do. They were raised with spanking and other punishment-based parenting methods as a means of control and "turned out okay" so they default to their own parents' choices without researching alternatives to spanking or considering whether "okay" could be improved upon.

Consider this, more than ninety-percent of American parents admit to spanking their children, and yet the common contention is that it's a decline in spanking that is responsible for the purportedly escalating rates of youth violence and crime. Is it really the less than ten-percent of children who aren't spanked who are responsible for all the problems of our society? Or could it be that the ninety-percent of children who are subject to violence at home in the form of being slapped, paddled, smacked, yanked, whipped, popped, spanked, etc. are taking those lessons out into the world? Is it just possible that children who are hit learn to hit? That children who are hurt learn to hurt? Perhaps the lesson they are learning is that 'might is right' and violence is the answer to their problems, the outlet for their stress, the route to getting others to do what they want.

People throughout history have complained about 'the trouble with kids today' and they've pinned all the ills of their society on supposedly permissive parenting. They've ranted about out-of-control children, disrespectful youth, entitlement, spoiling, disobedience, violence, self-centeredness, etc:

> *"The children now love luxury. They have bad manners, contempt for authority, they show disrespect to their elders.... They no longer rise when elders enter the room. They contradict their parents, chatter before company, gobble up dainties at the table, cross their legs, and are tyrants over their teachers."* ~Socrates, 5th Century BC

> *"What is happening to our young people? They disrespect their elders, they disobey their parents. They ignore the law. They riot in the streets inflamed with wild notions. Their morals are decaying. What is to become of them?"* ~Plato, 5th Century BC

> *"I see no hope for the future of our people if they are dependent on frivolous youth of today, for certainly all youth are reckless beyond words... When I was young, we were taught to be discreet and respectful of elders, but the present youth are exceedingly wise*

[disrespectful] and impatient of restraint"
~Hesiod, 8th Century BC

"The world is passing through troublous times. The young people of today think of nothing but themselves. They have no reverence for parents or old age. They are impatient of all restraint. They talk as if they knew everything, and what passes for wisdom with us is foolishness with them. As for the girls, they are forward, immodest and unladylike in speech, behavior and dress."
~Peter the Hermit, 13th Century AD

Sounds familiar, doesn't it? Maybe, though, there isn't really any 'trouble with kids today.' Maybe the problem is with parents who repeat the patterns their own parents set or with societies who view normal stages of development as somehow abnormal.

Maybe 'kids today' are just kids like they have been through the ages, full of exuberance and curiosity and learning their way in a great big world, and a listening ear, gentle guidance, and trusted arms to turn to when inevitable mistakes are made are really all children need to grow up into kind, helpful, responsible, productive members of our society.

The bottom line is that addressing our children's underlying needs, the actual causes of their behavior instead of just the behavior itself, is a far more effective parental approach as well as being significantly better for a healthy, mutually respectful parent/child relationship.

Let's send our children out into the world as adults with their needs met, with coping mechanisms in place for those times when the stresses overwhelm them, and with the knowledge of a safe haven where comfort is always available when the world hurts them. Let's learn how to seek solutions with our children instead of inflicting retributions on our children. And let's start sowing peace instead of violence in our homes and in the hearts of our children to make a better tomorrow for all of us. (*Two Thousand Kisses a Day: Gentle Parenting Through the Ages and Stages*)

"Peace I leave with you; my peace I give you. I do not give to you as the world gives. Do not let your hearts be troubled and do not be afraid."
John 14:27

Chapter 19

Fear Doesn't Lead to Faith:
Becoming Your Child's Safe Place

*"Truly I tell you, unless you change and become like little
children, you will never enter the kingdom of heaven."*
Matthew 18:3

....

"I need prayer to help me trust God."

"I need to learn to trust God more."

"I'm really struggling with trusting God."

Over and over and over in Christian circles we hear these prayer
requests and confessions. Again and again we try and struggle
and fail to trust God with our lives, our decisions, our hopes, our
dreams, our plans, our needs, our fears, our mistakes. We assign
accountability partners and prayer buddies to help each other in
our struggle to trust. We take classes and read books and attend
seminars. And yet still, we struggle and we fail and we wonder
why we find it so hard to trust.

Maybe the problem is that we aren't asking the right question,
though. Perhaps the question isn't, "Why can't we trust?" but
rather...

"How can we trust someone we've been trained not to trust?"

Consider this scene:

> *"Father: You didn't obey Daddy, did you?*
>
> *Child: No.*
>
> *Father: Do you remember what God says Daddy must
> do if you disobey?*

Child: Spank me?

Father: That's right. I must spank you. If I don't, then I would be disobeying God. You and I would both be wrong. That would not be good for you or for me, would it?

Child: No. (A reluctant reply) [4]

(Tedd Tripp, Shepherding a Child's Heart, p. 31)

"I have to hurt you to please God." That is the message this child hears. And, one day, this child will be an adult who asks for prayer to learn to trust, if he even wants a relationship with Someone he believes demands that he be hurt by those he loves most, Someone he has been *trained* to distrust.

Parents systematically breaking down a child's innate ability to trust simply makes no sense. The world will hurt, disappoint, and disillusion our children through the years, no doubt, but the brief season of childhood is a time to strengthen our children, not weaken them, and true strength is forged in gentleness, guided by wisdom, and steeped in peace. Our children need us to be their guardians, their protectors, their safe harbor in life's storms:

> Imagine a ship damaged at sea, broken and sinking fast, heading for the safety and shelter of the harbor only to be stopped at the end of the breakwaters, the line between storm-tossed sea and calm waters, and told to clean up their deck, fix their rudders, and examine their ship logs to see where they went wrong, all while still in danger of sinking in the rough seas.

> Now imagine a child, roughed up by his own bad choices or suffering at the hands of her own human weaknesses, hoping to find a safe harbor in a parent's healing embrace, but instead being punished, spanked, or sent to isolation in a corner or in their room…leaving them all alone in a stormy sea of human emotions when

what they really need in that moment is to reconnect with us. In their most difficult moments, they need our wisdom and guidance and the reassurance that, no matter what mistakes they make, no matter how badly they fail, no matter how far they fall, we will always, always be there to help them and heal them and forgive them and love them." (*Two Thousand Kisses a Day: Gentle Parenting Through the Ages and Stages*)

Isn't that what God offers us, even in *our* most difficult moments? Wisdom. Guidance. Reassurance. Forgiveness. Unconditional love.

"While we were yet sinners, Christ died for us." (Romans 5:8)

And yet isn't that what we have so much trouble trusting in as adults?

Trust and fear cannot coexist, and God certainly doesn't intend them to. That is why Jesus says over and over, *"Do not be afraid,"* throughout the New Testament. One stumbling block, though, is the use of the word 'fear' in translations of verses such as, *"The fear of the Lord is the beginning of wisdom," (Proverbs 9:10)* which lead us to believe that we must be afraid of God in order to honor him. But, while fear repels, wonder invites. The Hebrew word, *yirah*, which is translated 'fear' actually means, 'to see or be seen clearly' or 'to have a heightened awareness of' or 'to flow' as in 'to flow with overwhelming emotion.' In Hebrew, it is taken to mean 'to overflow with or be overcome by trepidation' only when used in the context of danger, but 'to overflow with or be overcome by awe and wonder' when used in the context of a good and mighty God. So, *"The fear of the Lord is the beginning of wisdom"* would more accurately read, *"Being overcome with awe and wonder at the Lord is the beginning of wisdom."*

Perhaps, if we parent our children the way God parents us, with mercy, understanding, and gentle guidance, our children's ability to trust will be strengthened rather than broken, and as adults they won't struggle to trust God as we so often do. Then, instead of running and hiding from God when life hits hard and the world batters and bewilders our children, perhaps they will go running *to* him, trusting that he will be there with outstretched arms, ready to heal their hurts, forgive their mistakes, and help them back on the right path.

In practical application, how does that look, though? How can we parent with mercy, understanding, and gentle guidance instead of with punishments and yet still manage to set and maintain reasonable boundaries and limits?

Here's an example of parenting without punishment, with mercy, understanding, and gentle guidance, from *Two Thousand Kisses a Day: Gentle Parenting Through the Ages and Stages* about how to handle lying:

> The line between fantasy and reality is very blurry for small children. They are convinced that they can talk to animals and can fly if they wear a cape and are faster runners if they wear their 'fast shoes.' They think that the moon follows them home and that if they stretch as tall as they can, they can touch the stars. It's one of the most beautiful and celebrated facets of the innocence of childhood, but also one of the most misunderstood.
>
> When a little boy puts a bowl on his head and makes up a fantastic story about rocketing to the moon in a cardboard spaceship, adults smile nostalgically and applaud his imagination. When that same little boy finds himself stuck in the uncomfortable position of being caught sneaking cookies from the pantry and makes up a story about the cookies accidentally falling off of the shelf into his mouth, those same adults often shame the child.
>
> When a little girl perches on the arm of the sofa and tells a tall tale about pirates and stormy seas and walking the plank, her parents will laugh and join in the fun, but that same child will often be punished if she spins a tale to cover her tracks after she stuffs a towel

down the toilet to see if it will flush and finds out that stuffed-up toilets overflow instead.

Communication is a complex skill, full of hidden nuances and subtle connotations and social mores that are far, far beyond the capacity of young children to understand. And yet they are often held to an impossible standard of perfection by the adults in their life.

Interestingly, those adults holding them to such a high standard rarely hold themselves to the same standard.

What adult, when faced with a traffic fine for speeding, hasn't protested that they didn't know they were going over the speed limit?

How often do adults say "I love your new haircut" or "You haven't aged a day" when the opposite is true?

How many adults call out of work sick when they aren't actually sick or return something to the store after using it and say it's unused or tell their spouse to say they aren't home when a phone call comes in they don't want to answer?

How, then, when adults are the ones modeling how communication should be used, can they expect children to somehow know instinctively when it is and isn't acceptable to lie? How can parents expect children to have the fortitude and maturity to simply accept the discomfort of telling the truth when they, themselves, so easily and so often lie to avoid their own discomfort?

And yet parents are often horrified and embarrassed when their child lies. So much so, in fact, that they react to their own emotions instead of responding appropriately to the child and the situation, and they end up shaming and/or punishing their child.

Think about it realistically for a moment, though. If children lie because they've seen the adults in their life lie, is shaming or punishing them fair? If they lie because they are uncomfortable and fearful, will making them more uncomfortable and fearful solve the problem? If they lie because it's normal for their developmental stage, does it seem reasonable to hold them accountable for it?

Having a few tools ready and available in your parenting 'toolbox' helps to avoid these ineffective and rather hypocritical adult reactions to children lying:

- First, be aware that the safer your children feel with you, the less likely they will be to lie. Removing the provocation of fear and discomfort will go a long way toward making your children trust you with the truth, no matter what it is.

- Second, even when children feel safe they may lie simply because small children often say how they wish things were and really believe they can make it happen just by saying it! Bearing this in mind can help you to see that innocent imagination at work that you enjoy so much in other settings and help you to exercise more patience and understanding.

- Third, when confronted with a lie, the best response is to calmly state the truth yourself, assure the child that they can always tell you the truth, and then move on without punishing the lie or giving the lie any more power or attention.

- Fourth, all behavior, including lying, is communication. Focusing on the need behind the behavior instead of the behavior itself or the lie it prompted will actually solve the problem rather than simply address the symptom of the problem.

- Fifth, keeping in mind that, over time, your children will mature enough to verbalize their needs instead of acting them out as long as their needs are met consistently and with understanding and respect while they are younger will help you to stay calm and focused. The end result will be healthy communication and trust with no need to lie.

Imagination truly is the language of childhood. It makes sense to try to understand their language instead of insisting they perfect ours. We are, after all, the only adults in the relationship.

Simply reacting to our children's behavior rather than responding to the need motivating the behavior not only leaves us in the dark as to what our children are thinking and feeling, but also misses an opportunity to address the root of the behavior. When we pause, breathe through our own visceral reactions, and focus on our child instead of our child's actions, we can better discern the need behind the behavior and meet that need, thus eliminating the behavior itself with no need for correction and opening the door to guiding our children to better ways of expressing themselves in the future. The end result is not only the resolution of the present issue, but also the strengthening of the parent/child relationship which gives our children the reassurance that they aren't alone in dealing with their stresses and questions and fears and can always come to us, their 'safe haven' in times of need. (*Whispers Through Time: Communication Through the Ages and Stages of Childhood*)

Trust is a two-way street. If our children know that they can trust us with their problems, their mistakes, their bad choices, their failures, then as they grow we will be able to trust them to come to us with those issues so that we can help them and guide them. And, if they've experienced a healthy trust relationship with us, their earthly parents, then their ability to trust God, their heavenly parent, will be strengthened instead of broken or damaged.

"There is no fear in love, but perfect love casts out fear, for fear has to do with punishment"
1 John 4:18

Chapter 20

Come, Let Us Reason Together

"In everything, do to others what you would have them do to you, for this sums up the Law and the Prophets."
Matthew 7:12

As parents, we have all most likely used the 'do unto others' line with our children a time or two, but how often do we stop and evaluate our own behavior to see if we are leading by example? Are we making sure to treat others how we'd like to be treated so that our children can see us living what we want them to learn? More importantly, are we treating our children how we, ourselves, like to be treated so that they see our faith in action in our own homes?

There is great truth to the idea that our children will learn far more from watching what we *do* than from listening to what we *say*. God's beautiful design demonstrates this reality in nature as mama ducks teach their ducklings to waddle and swim, and elephants cuddle and romp with their calves while teaching them to forage for food, and polar bears snuggle in snow caves with their young and teach them how to hunt and survive in the arctic temperatures.

Consciously, intentionally, and consistently living out how we want our children to turn out is the most powerful and effective guidance we can offer them. The lessons they take into the future will consist far more of how we treat them than what we teach them.

So, *"Come now, let us reason together" (Isaiah 1:18)* and let us look at some of the inconsistencies in how we treat our children:

- *demanding* respect because of our position but insisting children have to *earn* respect

- hitting to teach them not to hit

- teaching them that Jesus came to take the punishment for all, but that children must still be punished

- telling our children they must use self-control while trying to control them ourselves

- yelling at our children to stop yelling

- losing our temper because we're frustrated when our children have temper tantrums because they're frustrated

- insisting our children listen to us but not listening to our children

- wanting our children to come to us with their problems as teens but isolating them in time-out when they have a problem when they're toddlers

- telling them not to bottle up their emotions as teens after punishing them for not bottling up their emotions as toddlers

- telling them to use their gentle hands but not using ours

- gobbling grace for ourselves but not living it or giving it to our children

- insisting children can't learn without punishment then preaching the power of forgiveness

- demanding retribution and restitution if a child lies or breaks something but accepting freedom from accountability for our own bad choices and mistakes

- treating guests in our home with more patience and accommodation than the children with whom God has gifted us

- telling our struggling teen we're there for them day or night after leaving them alone in the dark as infants and toddlers

- accommodating our own tastes and preferences in food but not allowing them to have theirs

- needing downtime ourselves after a long day at work, but making them come straight home and do their homework

- not freely sharing everything we own with our friends and neighbors, but insisting that they share indiscriminately

- having a messy room but making them keep theirs clean

The fact is, parents, our children are watching how we live far more than they are hearing what we say. They are learning how to live by our choices, not by our words:

- We can lecture them eloquently about self-control, but if our children constantly see us angry and frustrated and yelling (i.e. lacking self-control), then that is what they'll internalize.

- We can preach daily sermons on honesty, but if our children see us lying to our supervisors ('cough, cough' "Sorry, I can't come in to work today. I'm sick…See you later, kids, I'm going fishing!") and cheating on our taxes, that's what they will learn.

- We can rhapsodize about the value of compassion, but if our children see us ignoring their needs in favor of our own, judging instead of helping those in need, and gossiping about others' pain, that is how they will learn to live.

- We can pontificate about respecting our fellow human beings, but if we constantly show disrespect for our children's feelings by shaming them or ignoring their preferences and opinions; or disrespect for their belongings by using their possessions as tools to manipulate, threaten, and control them; or disrespect for their person by yanking, hitting, or manhandling them, then that is how they will learn to treat others.

Pam Leo, author of *Connection Parenting*, wrote, "How we treat the child, the child will treat the world."

What our children learn from how we live is what they will take with them into the world. We must always ask ourselves if our lives reflect our faith, if our actions reflect our beliefs, and if how we treat our children is how we not only want to be treated, ourselves, but also how we want our children to treat the world.

"Therefore, as God's chosen people, holy and dearly loved, clothe yourselves with compassion, kindness, humility, gentleness and patience."
Colossians 3:12

Chapter 21

Sin

*"Therefore if you have any encouragement from
being united with Christ, if any comfort from his love, if any
common sharing in the Spirit, if any tenderness and compassion,
then make my joy complete by being like-minded, having the
same love, being one in spirit and of one mind."*
Philippians 2:1-2

What are your hearts' desires for your children, parents?
Happiness? Safety? Health? Wisdom? Salvation?

If we, as earthly parents, desire the best for our children and long
to keep them safe and happy and want them to trust us to take
care of them, why is it so hard to believe that God, as our
heavenly Parent, would desire the same for them? Are we really
better parents than God? Do we care more deeply and love more
fully than the One who gave everything for his children?

How much do we love our children?
He loves them more.

How much do we hurt for our children when they hurt?
He hurts more.

How much do we suffer for our children when they suffer?
He suffers more.

How much would we give to rescue them from the jaws of
death?
He's given more.

Sin disrupts God's relationship with his children and breaks his
heart, and yet he offers grace. Why do we have such a difficult
time doing the same?

Perhaps it's because our understanding of the words *discipline, sin, obedience, submission, subject to,* and *authority* has been skewed:

> *"Don't waste time trying to sugarcoat submission to make it palatable. Obeying when you see the sense in it is not submission; it is agreement. Submission necessarily means doing what you do not wish to do. It is never easy or painless."*[4] *(Tedd Tripp, Shepherding a Child's Heart, pg. 145)*

> *"Some have asked, "But what if the child only screams louder, gets madder?" Know that if he is accustomed to getting his unrestricted way, you can expect just such a response. He will just continue to do what he has always done to get his way. It is his purpose to intimidate you and make you feel like a crud pile. Don't be bullied. Give him more of the same. On the bare legs or bottom, switch him eight or ten licks; then, while waiting for the pain to subside, speak calm words of rebuke. If the crying turns to a true, wounded, submissive whimper, you have conquered; he has submitted his will. If the crying is still defiant, protesting and other than a response to pain, spank him again."*[17] *(Michael Pearl, To Train Up a Child, pg. 79)*

Some have said that God hates the sin but loves the sinner. I disagree. God doesn't hate the sin but love the sinner. He hates the sin *because he loves his child.*

The Old Testament Hebrew words most often translated 'sin' are *chata'ah* which means 'missing the mark' and *pasha* which means 'going beyond the limits.'[1,2,3] In Greek, found in the New Testament, the word most often translated 'sin' is *hamartia* which means, literally, 'not a part of' or 'has no share in.'[25] All in all, these words in their context in the original text of the Bible can be read, 'to miss God's mark, to go beyond God's limits, to not be a part of God's will.' Sin, then, is literally to depart from God, to operate outside of his nature.

These words convey a separation from God, and therein lies the crux of the issue. God is a Father who desperately loves his children, so desperately that he literally died to make a way for them to be with him for eternity. Sin makes him angry because it tears his children from his arms, but his anger is at the sin, not his children. His children are his delight, the subjects of his unconditional love.

'Discipline' means to teach, guide, instruct, and 'disciple' refers to a student or pupil.[26] In Chapter Eleven, we saw that the Hebrew word *muwcar* is translated 'discipline' in the Old Testament and means, literally, 'verbal instruction and teaching.'[1,2,3] In Hebrew culture *muwcar* was vernacular for 'let us reason with one another' implying a mutual discussion for learning purposes. In the New Testament, the Greek word *paideuo* is often translated 'discipline' or 'train,' but quite literally means 'nurture' as in to grow, nourish, and encourage.[25]

As an example, in the verse, *"But no discipline in its time seems to be joyful, but it is sorrowful; but in the end it yields the fruit of peace and of righteousness" (Hebrews 12:11)* the Greek word translated discipline is *paideuo* which means 'nurture' and 'instruction.' The Greek word translated 'sorrowful' or 'painful' is *lupe* which means to 'have one's conscience pained' or 'to regret' or even 'to labor' (as in childbirth, i.e. *"bring forth in sorrow" Genesis 3:16*). In context, this verse is referring to the trials and persecution some believers were experiencing because of their faith, and it is encouraging them to stay the course and reap the benefits of triumphing over hardships and obstacles. Literally, it is talking about God, as a father, allowing his children to experience the natural consequences of their behavior (all behavior, even desirable behavior, has consequences simply due to cause and effect). And it is also comforting them with the truth that God won't leave them in their times of trouble, but will help and support and guide them along the way.

'Obey,' as discussed in Chapter Seven, doesn't appear in the original text of the Bible.[24] The words translated 'obey' are (Hebrew) *hupakouo/hupakoe – to hear from above; to listen for;*

to lend an ear to; shama/lishmoa – to understand, to internalize, to ponder, to reflect upon[1,2,3] and (Greek) *peitho – to be persuaded; to be moved; to respond* which mean to listen and reflect, to thoughtfully consider, to respond positively.[25] So *"But if anyone obeys his word, love for God is truly made complete in them. This is how we know we are in him." (1 John 2:5)* reads *"But if anyone ~~obeys~~ understands, reflects upon, is persuaded by his word, love for God is truly made complete in them. This is how we know we are in him." (1 John 2:5)* It is a discourse, an interaction, an openness and closeness. It draws us near God in intimate communication.

'Submit,' *hupotasso* in New Testament Greek, means to choose to agree with, to walk in accord; to work together; to compromise; to be at peace[25]...it is an ongoing process between two or more people. Believers are called to submit to (agree with, be at peace with) each other several times in the Bible as in, *"~~Submit to~~ Agree with, compromise with, be at peace wtih one another out of reverence for Christ." (Ephesians 5:21)* Paul wasn't defining roles. He wasn't issuing commands. He was sharing relationship tips. Each person in a relationship needs to make sacrifices for the other. Each needs to think about the other's best good. He was saying that unity and fellowship come from intentional, voluntary, *mutual* give and take, *"There is no longer Jew or Gentile, slave or free, male and female. For you are all one in Christ Jesus." (Galatians 3:28)*

'Subject to' is the passive form of *hupotasso* and means to be in a relationship with, to be united with, to be as one.[25] It is not an action, but a relationship, a state of being, i.e. the relationship between God and his children, the relationship among a body of believers, the voluntary gathering and joining of lives, the 'kingdom of the heart,' the marriage relationship, the parent/child relationship.

For the Biblical definition of 'authority' we need look no further than Jesus. He was man. He is God. He is and was the ultimate authority. And he said, *"Even the Son of Man came not to be served but to serve." (Mark 10:45)* Authority, then, is not a hammer or a gavel or a whip. It is the gentle voice of a Servant-Savior calling, *"Come to me, all you who are weary and burdened, and I will give you rest. Take my yoke upon you and learn from me, for I am gentle and humble in heart, and you will find rest for your souls. For my yoke is easy and my burden is light."* (Matthew 11:28-30)

Let us follow Christ's example with our own children, then, parents. Let's walk in gentleness and understanding toward our children and invite them to walk alongside us as we navigate this joyful, chaotic, inspiring, crazy, beautiful life together.

> *"A new commandment I give to you, that you love*
> *one another, even as I have loved you,*
> *that you also love one another."*
> *John 13:34*

Chapter 22

A Heart of Forgiveness

"Put on then, as God's chosen ones, holy and beloved,
compassionate hearts, kindness, humility, meekness, and
patience, bearing with one another and, if one has a complaint
against another, forgiving each other; as the Lord has forgiven
you, so you also must forgive. And above all these put on love,
which binds everything together in perfect harmony."
Colossians 3:12-14

It often isn't until we become parents ourselves that our
childhood hurts begin to surface unexpectedly in outbursts of
anger toward our children or an inability to bond with our
children or a myriad of other subtle and not-so-subtle ways.

Working toward forgiveness and peace with our past is essential
so that we can stop the cycle and not pass along that baggage to
our children. Recognizing our childhood hurts and unmet needs,
isolating those feelings, and dealing with them with the adult
emotional maturity that we now have allows us to process,
forgive, and move on so that we don't repeat the past with our
own children.

That is easier said than done, but it is doable, and it is well worth
the emotional investment. Working through our childhood hurts
is about forgiving so that we can unload our baggage into the
past where it belongs instead of unloading it onto our children
and passing it along to the next generation. (*The Gentle Parent:
Positive, Practical, Effective Discipline*)

A peaceful response comes from a peaceful heart, so healing
from our past and present hurts and taking care of our own needs
is a vital step toward making sure that we can grow and guide
our children gently and peacefully. If we find ourselves reacting
to normal childhood behaviors with anger (yelling, threats,
intimidation, name-calling, manipulation, shaming, etc.) it may

be echoes of our past that are controlling us in the present. Recognizing that it is *our* emotions and experiences and expectations that are causing our outbursts and not our children's normal behaviors opens the door to making the changes necessary to grow into the kind of peaceful parents we want to be.

Anger is a safety valve, a catharsis of emotion. It takes the pain, the fear, the anguish that builds up inside of us, robbing our peace, festering and growing and invading our hearts and minds, and relieves the pressure in an eruption of negative emotion. That's why, even with the guilt we may feel after an eruption of anger, we still feel a temporary sense of peace, because for a moment, until the pressure begins to rebuild, we are free. To stop hurting our children with our flashes of rage, to stop bullying our children as we were bullied, and to stop repeating the negative patterns of our own past parenting mistakes, we must relieve the pressure *before* it explodes and free ourselves from the endless cycle of pain, anger, and guilt.

The key to freedom is forgiveness. Forgiveness empties the past of its power to empty the present of its peace. But it's a journey, an ongoing life-process, a day-by-day decision, not a destination. Also, forget about "forgiving and forgetting." Forgetting simply isn't possible. Humans cannot consciously erase their unconscious minds, and memories are stored in the deepest recesses of our minds. Holding ourselves to an impossible standard of "forgiving and forgetting" merely sets us up for failure. We can, though, take steps to color our memories of past hurts with the compassion that comes from seeing them through the lens of forgiveness.

Forgiveness is not only for the person who hurt us. They don't even need to be involved in the process, necessarily. Those who have hurt us may not deserve forgiveness, but we deserve the peace that forgiving them will bring. We forgive them to free ourselves, to release the past, and to move on. We don't always need to track them down and have a heart-to-heart or send them a letter or contact them at all. They may not be trustworthy enough to be a part of our lives again, so we don't need to invite them back in and take that chance if we choose not to. Forgiveness is, in a very significant way, for us, for our present and future happiness and, as parents, for our children's present and future happiness.

Keep in mind, though, that forgiveness isn't a stagnant well. It's a flowing river that must keep moving to keep healing. In other words, it isn't a one-time, forgive-and-forget moment. It's a process, a moment-by-moment choice that we make to let go and live fully, free from the chains of the past.

Forgiving someone doesn't mean telling them that hurting us was okay. It means telling ourselves that it's okay to stop hurting. It doesn't mean we have to trust them again. It means we can learn to trust ourselves again because we deserve it. It doesn't mean we have to give them a free pass back into our lives. It means we are free to take our lives back again. Forgiving is letting the hurts of the past go so that we can move freely into the future.

The flip side of the coin is forgiving ourselves for our own human mistakes. Self-forgiveness can be even more difficult than forgiving others, but it's just as important to release ourselves from the mistakes of the past so that we can move on into a brighter future. The thing to remember is that guilt is destructive, not constructive. Holding onto our guilt over past mistakes doesn't make up for those mistakes and it doesn't help us to avoid repeating those mistakes. In fact, just the opposite. Holding onto guilt keeps us in a constant state of pain which can then fester and either explode into angry outbursts (increasing our guilt and creating a vicious cycle of guilt/anger = more guilt/more anger, etc.) or may implode into self-destructive behaviors such as addictions, depression, self-harm, eating disorders, inability to feel love, etc. (also increasing guilt which increases the self-destructive behaviors).

Everyone has made decisions they regret, and, as parents, we have all reacted to our children in ways we wish we could take back. Looking at failure as an opportunity to learn helps us to forgive ourselves for our human moments and to equip ourselves with better parenting tools for the future. That, in turn, helps us to accept our children in their human moments and to guide them with gentleness and empathy to better ways of behaving in the future. Forgiving ourselves and learning from our inevitable mistakes transforms failure from a stumbling block into a stepping stone on our gentle parenting journey. (*Gentle Parenting Workshop 2: Healing from Your Past so You Don't Pass it Along to Your Children*)

We all have to accept our humanness and imperfections and just try to do better in the future. We are, after all, imperfect humans growing imperfect humans in an imperfect world, and that's perfectly okay. So let go of the guilt. It's not helping you or your children. Commit to forgive yourself for your mistakes and move on because only when you forgive yourself for *your* human moments will you be comfortable letting your children have *their* human moments.

Also, remember to take care of *you*. You are a person with real and valid needs. Underestimating the effects of exhaustion and unmet needs on your parenting is a common mistake that can lead to negative responses toward your children. As a result, your parenting can get so crowded with these unconscious reactions that your good intentions get lost. Just as a child's behavior reveals *their* underlying unmet needs, a parent's knee-jerk reactions reveal hidden needs and hurts that surface with stress or frustration. It isn't selfish to take care of your needs, so make time each day to give yourself a little tender loving care. (*Whispers Through Time: Communication Through the Ages and Stages of Childhood*)

When your reactions are no longer fueled by the hurts of the past, you can actually use your normal human emotions to fuel an empathetic response to your children. Frustration and annoyance are normal human emotions and, as such, are easily controllable when they aren't underpinned by exhaustion, pain, fear, etc. Pay close attention to the feelings that make you want to yell or threaten or lash out. Those feelings are where you can find the empathy you need to be able to exercise your 'grown-up' self-control and find ways to communicate with your children instead of shutting them down. When you recognize that the frustration making you want to yell or the annoyance making you want to lash out are the same feelings that are driving your children to cry or whine or scream or act out, your heart will automatically soften, and a gentle response is born.

If you begin to feel tense and overwhelmed, stop whatever you're doing, slow down, breathe, count to ten, take a brief break, do whatever you need to do to regain your adult control. Do a quick heart-check to see if you've picked up some of your past baggage and, if you have, walk yourself through the steps to lay it back down again. Then ask yourself what the next step in your day needs to be, not the next ten steps, just the next step, and then take it. (*Gentle Parenting Workshop 2: Healing from Your Past so You Don't Pass it Along to Your Children*)

One helpful tool is a touchstone in a color that will help to keep you grounded, something to look at or hold on to when you feel yourself slipping back into old thinking and behavior patterns. It could be a necklace or bracelet or key chain in a color that captures the essence of the parent you want to be to help you stay focused as you work your way toward becoming that parent. Colors have psychological implications, so some good choices might be blue which is the color of peace and trust; turquoise which is the color of communication; pink which is the color of unconditional love; or magenta which is the color of harmony.[41] You can also place the color around your house as a reminder of the peaceful home you're trying to create and as a symbol of change and renewal to help you remember to stop and breathe and think before responding to your children. (*The Gentle Parent: Positive, Practical, Effective Discipline*)

Above all, keep in mind that you are blazing a new trail, both for yourself and your children. Give yourself and your children the room to make mistakes and to learn from those mistakes. Remember…

> Parenting has nothing to do with perfection. Perfection isn't even the goal, not for us, not for our children. Learning together to live well in an imperfect world, loving each other despite or even because of our imperfections, and growing as humans while we grow

our little humans, those are the goals of gentle parenting. So don't ask yourself at the end of the day if you did everything right. Ask yourself what you learned and how well you loved, then grow from your answer. That is perfect parenting. (*Gentle Parenting Workshop 1: Getting Started on Your Gentle Journey*)

Here are some steps you can take to move away from a punitive parenting style to one characterized by compassion, kindness, and gentleness:

So few parents today were raised peacefully and respectfully by their own parents that it's no surprise that a big issue in the gentle parenting community is how to overcome the stumbling blocks of change. Moving from a control-based parenting style, whether you're used to spanking or time-outs or reward charts or some combination of the three, to a connection-based parenting style is a heart and mindset change as much as it is a lifestyle change. The undeniable fact is that change is hard work. Whether you're trying to overcome your own childhood or your own already-established parenting habits, you can expect it to get harder before it gets easier. Just like with any lifestyle change, you will hit walls along the way, and they might even knock you back a step or two. Here are five tips to help you keep calm and carry on to achieve your parenting goals:

1. Commit to no hitting or other physical expressions of anger or frustration, and let that be your starting point, the line in the sand that you absolutely will not cross. Just like in marriage, if you don't make a commitment, there's nothing to keep you from straying back into old patterns.

2. Rethink your parenting role and move away from trying to force or manipulate or plead or coerce or use any other tactic to try to control your child's behavior and instead build a desire in your child to cooperate because they trust you to make good

decisions and to want them to be happy and safe. Do that by taking all of that energy that's been going into trying to control their behavior (external controls) and focusing it on trying to build your connection and modeling the behavior you want to encourage (building internal controls).

3. Examine what you're modeling. If right now you are insisting on your own way and reacting emotionally with anger and power-plays to your child's lack of cooperation, what are you modeling? Stubbornness and lack of emotional regulation (i.e. adult-style tantrums). If, instead, you connect with your child, engage them in creative problem-solving, and work together with them toward a resolution to whatever issue you're having, what are you modeling? Compromise, resourcefulness, and cooperation. Definitely worthwhile life lessons!

4. Keep working on *you*. Remind yourself that it's *your* emotions and experiences and expectations that are causing your outbursts, not your little one's behavior. Ask yourself why you're so upset. Explore your inner triggers. Work through that internally instead of reacting to it externally.

5. Don't forget to choose a touchstone, as mentioned earlier in this chapter, in a color that will help to keep you focused on the relationship you are building with your child and on the parent you are working toward becoming.

Remember, it's a huge change to go from demanding obedience to inviting cooperation, and if you are already in an adversarial pattern with your child, that process will take extra time and patience. And keep in mind that no parenting 'works' to change a child into an adult or into a perfect little puppet. Children are children, as they should be. But shifting your thinking from expecting, or demanding, obedience to working with your child, understanding them, connecting with them, and inviting them to cooperate (i.e. Instead of "If you don't put your dinner dishes in the sink, you won't get ice cream for dessert" try "Let me know when your dishes are in the sink so I can get your ice cream for you.") is the first and most important step toward a gentler style of parenting and a more peaceful home. (*The Gentle Parent: Positive, Practical, Effective Discipline*)

> *"Therefore, there is now no condemnation*
> *for those who are in Christ Jesus."*
> *Romans 8:1*

Chapter 23

Fearfully and Wonderfully Made

"I praise you because I am fearfully and wonderfully made;
your works are wonderful, I know that full well."
Psalm 139:14

The Hebrew word translated 'fearfully' is *yirah*, which means,
literally, 'to see or be seen with intense clarity and intentionality,
to have a heightened awareness of, to flow with emotion.'[1,2,3] So
Psalm 139:14 (above) could also be read, *"I praise you because
you saw me clearly, made me intentionally, and formed me
wonderfully."* The connotation of that 'seeing' and 'being seen'
is a mutual wonder, amazement, and awe, on our part at what
God has done, and on God's part at the beauty of his creation. It
implies an intimate, intentional knowing, a relationship between
the Creator and the created, a joy-filled Father and a wonder-
filled child. It conveys the intricate precision with which God
hand-crafts each of his children as an artist tenderly conceives,
finely sculpts, and meticulously paints his masterpiece. And, it
communicates the studied design of a master craftsman
singularly designing each individual to be as distinct and diverse
as snowflakes, with no two ever exactly alike.

Consider...

> The artistry and creativity of childhood extends far
> beyond stray crayon marks on walls, masterpieces hung
> on refrigerators, and colorful macaroni necklaces.
> Children are unique individuals with their own
> distinctive outlooks and perspectives. Each brings
> special gifts to the world that parents have the
> opportunity to nurture and inspire during the short
> season of childhood.

Watching our children blossom and become their own person is fascinating, but may be a bit disconcerting when their personalities and perspectives are significantly different from ours. Learning how to communicate with them effectively is the key to working with, instead of against, their uniqueness.

Sometimes that key to effective communication can be found in observing how our children observe the world. The artist in each child has a wonderfully unique perspective:

The Photographer is the child who captures the world in still shots, moments etched in their minds like photographs in an album, telling them who we are, who they are, what the world is like. This child defines the world in individual experiences, categorizing them, labeling them, and filing them away for future reference. Communicating with them is often most effective when centered around shared experiences, both good and bad. Conversations with The Photographer typically begin with, "Remember when...?"

The Painter is the child who sees the world in broad strokes, creating mental canvases of ever-changing hue and texture. This child often defines the world in ideals and possibilities rather than realities. Communicating with them tends to be most effective when phrased in language that supports their ideals while gently helping them to cope with reality. Conversations with The Painter often start with, "What if...?"

The Sculptor is the child who explores the world by chipping away at it, uncovering its dimensions and discovering its potential a layer at a time. This child defines the world in a series of challenges, digging and testing and pushing to find out the depth and breadth and possibility inherent in each moment, each person, each experience. Communicating with them is often most effective when their quest for knowledge is addressed first, before any attempt is made to redirect or correct. Conversations with The Sculptor tend to start with, "Why...?"

Embracing our children's perspective, taking the time to really know and appreciate them as individuals, communicating and connecting with them, and guiding them through childhood in an atmosphere of acceptance and unconditional love will free the artist in each of them to share their remarkable and unique beauty with the world.

Seeing the world through the lens of the artist in each of our children not only helps us to communicate and connect with them, but also gives us the gift of seeing the world through the eyes of a child again. And, when our children have different personalities and perspectives from our own, as challenging as that can be as parents, seeing the world through their artistic lens may be an entirely new and eye-opening experience for us and broaden our understanding of the world in unexpected ways. Thus, the challenge becomes the gift, as is so often true in life. (*Whispers Through Time: Communication Through the Ages and Stages of Childhood*)

Of course, recognizing that our children are as individual as snowflakes and understanding their particular perspective, how they think and feel and interact with the world, are two distinct issues in and of themselves. Part of the joy of being a parent is in the discovery of who our little individuals are and in the wonder of watching them and the privilege of guiding them as they grow and learn and explore this lovely world God has given us. But helping them navigate the normal ups and downs of childhood can be challenging if we don't have a good sense of who our children were created to be when it comes to personality, communication style, and outlook. Examining some of the traits that characterize children as introverted or extroverted, as dreamers or doers, as observers or participants, can help us to interact with our children more effectively and relate to them more intentionally:

> From tantrums to whining to tattling to the endless 'why's,' the evolution of children's communication proceeds at a steady and relatively predictable pace, though the timing is influenced by factors such as individual personality, cognitive development, home environment, etc. Once children have a solid grasp of language and have developed more advanced reasoning and processing skills, and once they've examined the in's and out's of their parents' thoughts and beliefs, they begin to turn their attention to discovering their *own* interests and gifts and personalities.

> Parents often begin to notice their children 'becoming their own person' during this time and we hear laments such as "She's eight going on eighteen" and "He's already changed career plans four times, and he's only ten!" It is during this period in childhood that children often develop into a chatterbox or a dreamer, though most will be unique combinations of the two.

> When you have a chatterbox, whether you have a seven-year-old who could seemingly spend entire days describing every super hero's powers, weapons, weaknesses, enemies, and transportation or a nine-year-old who can list every horse breed, how to handle grooming, and what type of equipment to use for each kind of riding, the endless chattering can be deafening. The common theme is exploring who they are and what they like and what they think, all of which is accompanied by an intense need to share this fascinating process with the people they respect and admire the most…their parents, teachers, grandparents, siblings, anyone they've built a strong trust relationship with in their earlier years.

> Chatterboxes can be challenging, to say the least. The never-ending talking, the intensity of their focus, and the often fickle nature of their passion (just when you

get used to the daily commentary on the virtues of all things aquatic, their interest shifts and you're getting a lesson in martial arts that would make an encyclopedia look dumb!) can really keep you off-balance.

A common problem parents encounter at this stage is dealing with how to encourage their children in their interests without pushing them. So often when a child expresses interest in music their parent immediately buys a trumpet and enrolls him in lessons only to find that their budding Louis Armstrong has suddenly decided music is for the birds. His interests have flown elsewhere, and he's now too busy pursuing his new passion for veterinary medicine to bother with something so pedantic as practicing the trumpet!

While encouraging our children to follow through on their commitments is important, we need to let them lead the way as much as possible. One way to avoid this situation is to make sure that we aren't jumping into things too quickly rather than giving our children a chance to explore their interests unhindered by the demands and pressures of lessons and competitions.

The constant nature of the chatterbox's chattering can be grating on parental nerves, to be sure. However, not only allowing, but actually encouraging, our chatterboxes to share their thoughts as they begin to navigate the *"Who am I? What inspires me? What will I be?"* stage is important for a number of reasons:

- First, for a chatterbox, the need to be heard is intense, and it's a wise parent who meets that need. Not only does remaining open and available at this stage continue to build the trust that is so vital for a respectful and peaceful relationship, but it also sets the stage for healthy communication in the rapidly approaching teen years.

- Second, a child who is heard and encouraged in discovering themselves at this stage tends to enter adolescence a more well-grounded and focused individual. Young people who head into the teen years without having begun the process of self-discovery in middle childhood are more likely to be rudderless and vulnerable to peer pressure.

- Third, there is a unique window of clarity, a 'honeymoon' so to speak, in the middle years of childhood wherein language skills have been acquired, cognitive processes have matured, and the clouding of adolescent hormones and pressures and outside relationships aren't in the mix to muddy the waters. This is prime real estate for encouraging self-discovery while parental wisdom still seems wise to a child.

On the other end of the spectrum of middle childhood is the dreamer. Some children become extraordinarily introspective during this period. They are often lost in thought and may be perceived as inattentive or withdrawn. Oddly, it may seem harder to parent a dreamer because, while we rarely have to wonder what's going on in the mind of a chatterbox, it takes a constant, subtle level of awareness to stay in tune with a young dreamer. That awareness is vital, though, because your young dreamer still needs your attention and empathetic support and guidance, just in different ways.

Some of the subtleties to be aware of are:

- Signs of discomfort in social situations that they may not verbalize, but that we can offer insights into or alternatives to

- Signs of anxiety such as frequent headaches or

stomach aches which could be non-verbal cues that need our attention

- Watching for what topics inspire their interest so we can encourage them on their road to self-discovery

Checking in frequently with a dreamer is important since they may not volunteer information.

Asking questions such as *"That must have been difficult. Would you like to talk about it?"* and *"I feel like you're struggling with that. Can I help?"* along with observations such as *"You seem to find that interesting"* are discussion openers they may or may not take you up on, but let them know you care.

Don't push them to open up, though, by constant probing questions or being unwilling to follow their lead if they aren't ready to talk. Just create the opportunity for conversation and, if possible, do so at regular intervals and in a quiet place so that they know they can count on a private time to share when they are ready.

Prepare to simply sit in companionable silence during these times so your young dreamer won't feel rushed or pressured, but don't be surprised if they occasionally transform into a chatterbox and let all their pent up passions pour out at once before drifting back into their inner world.

*Note: It is important to be aware of the subtle signs that can differentiate a dreamer from a withdrawn, angry, or depressed child. While a dreamer may often be in their own little world, it tends to be a happy world. If your child seems sad, is overly irritable, has trouble concentrating, seems unusually tired, becomes extremely sensitive to and negatively affected by social situations, etc. then it may be wise to seek a professional evaluation.

While the chatterbox and dreamer stage may be just that, a stage, and your child may grow out of the extroversion or introversion they appear to exhibit during this time, it's still helpful to examine the differences between those two personalities and find the best ways to communicate and interact with them.

Here is a breakdown of the two ends of the extrovert/introvert spectrum to help you get a feel for your child's personality:

Introverts:

- tend to think before they speak
- typically don't talk much
- are often uncomfortable in crowds
- tend to speak quietly and thoughtfully
- avoid the limelight
- tend to stick with an activity or conversation until it's finished
- often prefer written communication
- are often indecisive
- tend to be cautious
- tend to be shy or reserved
- often have one or two close friends
- tend to be focused, sometimes to the point of obsession
- are often serious
- tend to be thinkers

Extroverts:

- often like the limelight
- typically are comfortable in crowds
- often speak loudly and quickly
- tend to interrupt
- often have poor impulse control
- often jump from one activity to another
- tend to have trouble finishing tasks

- often think out loud
- tend to jump to conclusions
- are often decisive
- tend to be leaders
- are often easily distracted
- tend to be energetic and enthusiastic
- often are surrounded by friends
- tend to be doers

Once you have an idea what personality tendencies your child has, there are some key elements to consider when offering guidance and trying to communicate with them.

Introverts:

- often need a moment to think before responding to questions or requests
- need privacy when learning new skills
- respond more positively to guidance and praise when offered in private
- often need support when entering new situations
- tend to respond better to change when it is discussed in advance
- often need time to redirect their attention when absorbed in an activity
- don't respond well to being pushed into interacting with strangers
- often have a great need to have their personal space respected

Extroverts:

- tend to respond well when offered choices
- often need lots of physical affection and roughhousing
- respond better to independent exploration than guided teaching
- like to be complimented openly and publically

- need the freedom to try new things even when they haven't finished other things
- tend to work well in groups
- often still need time to redirect their attention when absorbed in an activity

These characteristics and suggestions aren't exhaustive, but they are springboards you can use to understand and communicate with your own unique 'snowflake' more intimately, effectively, and intentionally. (*Whispers Through Time: Communication Through the Ages and Stages of Childhood*)

"There are different kinds of spiritual gifts, but the same Spirit is the source of them all."
1 Corinthians 12:4

Chapter 24

The Power of Kindness

*"Be kind to one another, tenderhearted, forgiving one another,
as God in Christ forgave you."*
Ephesians 4:32

There is a mistaken belief that kindness equals weakness, but
nothing could be further from the truth. Let's not mistake
toughness with strength. Kindness, compassion, and generosity
come from a strength of character that runs soul-deep.
Toughening is hardening. It creates callouses under which a
wounded heart bleeds beneath layers of scar tissue. A tough
person is a hurting person, and hurting people tend to hurt
people, not necessarily intentionally, but because they react out
of their pain instead of from a heart of peace. True strength is
forged in gentleness, guided by wisdom, and steeped in peace. A
strong person is a heart-whole person, and wholeness begets
wholeness just as kindness begets kindness, compassion begets
compassion, strength begets strength, and peace begets peace.

In *Whispers Through Time: Communication Through the Ages
and Stages of Childhood* I wrote, "It's not our job to toughen our
children up to face a cruel and heartless world. It's our job to
raise children who will make the world a little less cruel and
heartless."

In response, many people have asked how our children will be
able to withstand the harsh realities of life if they haven't been
toughened up at home in preparation. The answer lies in the
power of human connection. The safety and security and healthy
relationships that children experience at home are what
strengthen them and prepare them to not just withstand those
harsh realities, but to actively work to change those realities.

Humans are relational, designed by God for a relationship with himself. We learn about that relationship through our earthly relationships, mainly our relationship with our parents. Healthy relationships in childhood prepare children for healthy relationships as adults, not only with God, but with others, as well. When children are treated with kindness, respect, and compassion, they are far more likely carry the seeds of kindness, respect, and compassion into the world with them and plant them in the hearts and lives of others they meet on their journey through life.

Additionally, our children's experiences in childhood strongly influence how they will view and interact with the world. Children learn through their experiences far more than they do from simply hearing about or reading about others' experiences. When they are toddling around getting into everything, they are learning. When they are in the climbing and exploring stage, they are learning. When they are in the 'why' stage, they are learning. When they are in the peer stage, they are learning. And, through it all, the safety and security and connection they feel with their parents, or the lack thereof, will determine how much influence and guidance their parents will have in their development. Whether they are encouraged to grow and discover and play and learn or they are contained, restrained, and constrained, childhood is the fertile soil in which they will grow into the adults we will send out into the world:

> Many parents misinterpret normal, childlike behaviors as unwanted intruders, weeds to be plucked, poisoned, and prevented so their little ones can flourish in the hothouse of childhood. What they don't realize is that childhood isn't a hothouse to be fenced in and closed off and climate-controlled. It's a wide-open, sun-drenched, wind-swept field of endless possibilities, experiences, and discoveries. And normal, childlike behaviors are the tumult of brilliant wildflowers sharing their vivid beauty in the riotous yellows of children shrieking and running in the sunshine, the gorgeous blues of children splashing in the sea, the stunning

silver sparks of eyes lighting up in discovery, and the lovely purples of laughter floating on an afternoon breeze. They linger for an all-too-brief season before they're gone forever, lost in the business and busyness of adulthood.

This focus on weeding out normal behaviors seems ingrained in our modern rush-through-life mentality which has parents racing to correct behaviors and to push their children to reach developmental milestones and to force early independence. The thing is, though, that given time, independence will grow naturally on its own. Developmental milestones will be reached in a child's own unique timetable. Communication through behavior will evolve into verbal communication in its time.

Imagine how much conflict could be eliminated if we simply connected with our children where they are rather than pushing them to be where they aren't, if we listened with our hearts, provided guidance and understanding, modeled desired behaviors, and offered help when our children struggled.

Imagine how much more we, as parents, could enjoy our children's childhood if we took the time to see the world anew through our children's eyes, to appreciate the beauty inherent in the small moments of life, and to find our own childlike joy renewed as we discover again the ability to wonder as we revisit our own childhood to learn new truths about life, about ourselves, about the world.

Imagine those most precious gifts of parenting that we miss in our rush through life, those breathtaking moments of extraordinary joy a child finds in the most ordinary discoveries that can never be recaptured—the priceless first taste of a strawberry, the wonder of a butterfly's wings, the giggle at a kitten's batting paws, the belly laugh at a playmate's silly joke, the pride of a first bicycle ride, the excitement of a home run, the awe of a first loose tooth.

These are gifts our children long to share with us... if we'll only take the time to slow down and join them in the timeless, but oh-so-brief, moments of childhood.

Instead, though, we often methodically, albeit unknowingly, deny our children a childhood with our pushing and rushing and unreasonable expectations, and then we wonder why we have so many behavior issues with them. Even if our discipline approach is gentle, if we aren't letting our children be children, then we are missing the heart of gentle parenting entirely. Knowing our children, staying in-tune with their needs, nurturing their uniqueness, growing them into who they were created to be instead of molding them into who we want them to be, these are the tenets of gentle, respectful, responsive parenting.

Our children are children for such a small season of life. Let their laughter ring out, their imaginations soar, their feet stomp in puddles, their hands clap for joy. Too soon they will grow up and out of their youthful exuberance and zest and settle into the life and routine of adulthood. Don't make them settle too soon. (*The Gentle Parent: Positive, Practical, Effective Discipline*)

Growing our children into kind, compassionate, respectful adults doesn't stop with letting them fully experience the joys of childhood, though. Maintaining our connection with them is part and parcel of maintaining our influence and ability to effectively guide them through the ups and downs of childhood:

From kicking and rolling and stretching to being lulled to sleep by the rhythmic cadence of a mama's heartbeat, little ones spend the first months of their existence wrapped in a warm, dark, gently swaying cocoon, a life-giving embrace, the ultimate hug, readying themselves for their grand entrance into the world.

Then, in those first moments of life beyond the womb, when the muffled sounds of the outside world become clear and the muted lights become glaringly bright, a warm breast with the sweet scent of life-sustaining milk and the soothing sound of a familiar heartbeat welcome the little one to the comfort and safety of a mama's arms.

In the days, weeks, and months that follow, little fingers and toes are counted and kissed again and again and again. Soft cheeks are snuzzled, and a fuzzy little head is nuzzled, and two thousand kisses a day seems a reasonable number to a parent's heart overflowing with tenderness for this tiny new member of the family.

Then comes the rolling and sitting and crawling and walking, and soon the two thousand kisses a day dwindle to brief morning cuddles before a toddler is off to explore the world, healing kisses on boo-boos, and goodnight snuggles with a bedtime book.

Time passes and little ones grow in independence, getting up and dressed and ready on their own, grabbing their own bandage for a scrape, and reading themselves to sleep. Gone are the snuzzles and nuzzles of infancy, and the two thousand kisses a day are simply sweet memories.

Growing independence, though, doesn't have to mean growing separation. Humans were created to be relational beings. We may outgrow our dependency, but we never outgrow the need for community, interaction, appreciation, reassurance, and support.

Infants, children, and adults alike all share this life-long need for connection. Over time that need will also be met through friendships, business engagements, social interactions, and the like; but family relationships are the steady and sure bedrock of secure connection and belonging that ground us and assure us that our needs will not go unmet even in the darkest of times.

Meeting that human need for secure connection is what gentle parenting is all about. Unfortunately, gentle, attachment-style parenting is often misconstrued to be simply about breastfeeding, babywearing, and co-sleeping. But, while those are possible choices for creating a secure parent/child connection in the early years, they are just a small sampling of the relationship-building and relationship-maintaining choices that parents can make throughout their children's lives.

As little ones outgrow the 'two thousand kisses a day' stage, parents can begin consciously creating 'two thousand connection points a day' to replace those tender expressions of love with age-appropriate expressions of appreciation and approval, love and support.

From responding empathetically to a preschooler's whine, to paying attention to a seven-year-old when they tell their endless stories, to listening 'between the lines' to the angst of a teen, maintaining a secure parent/child connection beyond infancy is simply about meeting emotional needs consistently, intentionally, and relationally.

Creating two thousand connection points a day isn't about quality time, and it isn't even about the quantity of time spent with our children. It is, instead, about being there in the small moments, the moments that matter to our children, and consciously meeting with them right where they are. It is about...

- Simply smiling and letting our eyes light up with welcome when our children walk into the room

- Maintaining eye contact when our children talk to us instead of letting our eyes constantly stray back to our laptops or cell phones or televisions

- Voicing our sincere appreciation for their latest 'masterpiece,' victory, or achievement

- Expressing our affection physically in whatever way our children are comfortable with, whether it's a dog-pile-on-daddy wrestling match, a knuckle pound, or a hug

- Giving our children our undivided, wholehearted attention when they share their latest treasure or sing a never-ending song they make up as they go or just want to sit and be close for awhile

- Listening to what our children need to say without them feeling the threat of repercussion

- Inferring what they aren't able to express verbally

- Inviting our children into our daily lives, whether we are discussing politics or cooking dinner or fixing the car

- Allowing our children to express their emotions, even when those emotions aren't pretty

- Validating their anger, hurt, frustration, or embarrassment instead of minimizing or dismissing their feelings

- Helping them to process their emotions by listening to them and reflecting back what we hear

- Guiding them toward the understanding of their own feelings and empathetically equipping them with coping mechanisms for the future

- Sharing our own hurts, disappointments, and mistakes in age-appropriate terms so they'll know it's okay to be human

- Honoring our children's intense need to avoid embarrassment by offering guidance privately and respectfully, even if their behavior issue is public and/or disrespectful

- Sharing their interests even if the life-cycle of a snail wouldn't be our first choice of dinner conversation

- Offering choices so they can grow in independence and confidence

- Supporting them even when their choices lead to disappointment or failure

- Being gently and kindly and completely honest about our own disappointment or hurt when their behavior negatively affects us, so they'll know they can trust us to be truthful, even in the hard things

- Helping them whenever and wherever they express a need for assistance so they'll know they never have to cope with life alone

These connection points are about maintaining and enriching a strong parent/child relationship through all of the ages and stages of childhood so that, through a foundation of trust and mutual respect, parenting takes the form of guiding instead of punishing, encouraging natural growth instead of forcing premature independence, and creating a strong, intimate, interwoven family fabric that will stand the test of time.

We must always keep in mind, though, that gentle parenting is a journey, not a destination. From the first awareness that a new life is growing, through infancy, toddlerhood, the preschool years, middle childhood, the teen years, and on into young adulthood, we are learning to be parents in the boots-on-the-ground, learn-as-we-go school of parenthood. No matter how prepared we are, there will always be unexpected challenges as surely as there will be unexpected joys, and we will always need to be willing to stretch and grow and learn. (*Two Thousand Kisses a Day: Gentle Parenting Through the Ages and Stages*)

Growing kind children starts at home by being kind *to* our children. Gentleness, faithfulness, and self-control have their roots at home, in *our own* behavior. Joy and peace are flowing springs that we can share with our children to grow them into healthy adults who will change the world instead of being changed by the world. The adults we send out into the world will reflect the love, joy, peace, patience, kindness, goodness, faithfulness, gentleness, and self-control they experience from us at home.

"'Love the Lord your God with all your heart and with all your soul and with all your strength and with all your mind'; and, 'Love your neighbor as yourself...'Which of these three do you think was a neighbor to the man?'... The expert in the law replied, 'The one who had mercy on him.' Jesus told him, 'Go and do likewise.'"
Luke 10:27-28 & 37

Chapter 25

Raising Peacemakers:
Stepping Up and Standing Down

"Blessed are the peacemakers: for they shall
be called the children of God."
Matthew 5:9

"When you are met with excuses or explanations, they
are not obeying. When they refuse to respond at once,
they are not obeying...You must challenge disobedience
and persevere until the lessons of submission are
learned. Victory does not come to the faint of heart.
Never allow your children to disobey without dealing
with them."[4] (Tedd Tripp, Shepherding a Child's Heart,
p. 139)

Responding to our children's challenging behaviors with
challenging behaviors of our own is not only simply throwing
fuel on a fire, it's also the polar opposite of the call to be
peacemakers, to be imitators of Christ who, even from the Cross,
whispered words of peace, comfort, and forgiveness. Our
children are children, even in their teens, and they are learning
from us how to handle conflict and disagreements. The last thing
most parents want their children to learn is that 'might makes
right' and that powering up on a smaller, younger person is
acceptable for any reason.

Of course, that begs the question, "What can we do when faced
with defiance and backtalk from our children?"

The answer can be found as discussed before in the Three C's of
gentle discipline: Connection, Communication, and mutual

Cooperation and in those three all-important phrases, "I'm here. I hear you. How can I help?"

Consider…

>   With more than 90% of parents admitting to spanking
>   or otherwise physically punishing their children at least
>   occasionally, mainstream American parenting can
>   certainly be defined as punitive. If you go to the library
>   or browse the shelves at Barnes & Noble or check out
>   Amazon's best sellers in the parenting genre, you will
>   find a predominance of popular, punishment-based,
>   obedience-focused parenting guides. Whether its
>   spanking or time-outs or removal of privileges or being
>   confined in their room, the vast majority of children in
>   the United States are raised with punitive parenting.
>
>   When it comes to children talking back to parents,
>   many of these punitive parenting guides dictate a zero-
>   tolerance policy. By their definition, backtalk is often
>   characterized as verbal or emotional abuse of parents,
>   defiance, rudeness, or threats:
>
>   - Verbal or emotional abuse of parents is
>   considered any statement that insults or hurts a
>   parent such as, *"You're so mean!"* or *"I wish I
>   didn't even have parents!"* or *"I hate you!"*
>
>   - Defiance is any statement containing the word
>   *"No"* in response to a parental command.
>
>   - Rudeness is defined as anything from deep
>   sighs to rolled eyes to stomped feet.
>
>   - Threats are any statements that give conditions
>   such as, *"If you take away my cell phone, I'll
>   just go get a new one!"* or *"If you don't drive
>   me to my friend's house, I'm walking there!"*
>
>   These parenting guides direct parents to decide which
>   punishment to mete out when their child talks back to

them, specifying that the deciding factor should be whichever punishment would be the most unpleasant, painful, and distressing for the child. Punishments are to be carried out swiftly and without discussion. When the retribution for the child's actions is over, it is to be followed with a lecture laying down the laws of the family. Again, no discussion is allowed, but if the child expresses appropriate penitence, love and hugs can then be offered.

In addition to the sick feeling in the pit of my stomach at the thought of children being subjected to this kind of harsh, punitive parenting, I'm saddened by the upside-down reasoning that shuts communication down instead of utilizing it to bring healing, understanding, and restoration to the parent/child relationship.

Take a look at the order of parenting prescribed: First, *punishment* meted out by the parent. Second, *lecture* delivered by the parent. Third, *conditional reconnection* based on a proper expression of remorse to the parent from the child.

In gentle parenting, the order and intent of parenting would be the polar opposite: First would come *listening* for the need behind the behavior and reconnecting with the child at the point of need. Second, would be initiating a two-way *communication* about the problem and brainstorming about how to address the issue in ways that will meet everyone's needs. Third, would be offering *guidance* and equipping the child with better ways to express needs in the future.

The punitive parenting approach focuses on the child *as* the problem and attempts to solve the problem by 'fixing' the child through intentionally unpleasant external forces.

The gentle parenting approach focuses on the child *having* a problem and attempts to help the child solve the problem through connection, communication, and inviting cooperation.

Now look at the definitions of backtalk--verbal and emotional abuse of parents, defiance, rudeness, and threats. The questions that immediately arise are: What about the parents? Are they held to the same standards as the children? Or do they threaten? Do they say 'No'? Do they sigh? Do they hurt their children?

As parents, our actions will always be reflected in our children's behavior. Children learn what they live. No amount of lecturing can undo the powerful impact on a child of their parent's own behavior and choices.

When a child backtalks, sometimes also referred to as mouthing-off or sassing, they are in the throes of a huge, internal maelstrom of emotion. Whatever they are reacting to in the moment, whether it's being told 'no' about something or being asked to do or not do something, it is rarely *those* issues that are at the root of the problem. The moment at hand is just the tipping point causing a fissure in the child's heart that lets out a bit of the steam inside. The real concern should be that there is, metaphorically, steam in the child's heart to begin with.

It is at this point that parents have the opportunity to model self-control and self-regulation by controlling their own knee-jerk reaction to their child's backtalk. Instead of meeting fire with fire, childish outburst with childish parental outburst, child's tantrum with adult tantrum, parents can slow down, breathe through their own emotions, and then listen through the fiery storm of their child's words to the hurt, fear, and anger behind the words.

In the same way that *"a gentle answer turns away wrath," (Proverbs 15:1)* a soft-voiced, *"Let's take a minute and calm down so we can work through this together, okay?"* from a parent is a magical, healing balm that immediately begins to diffuse tough situations and creates an atmosphere in which connection and communication can bring effective, peaceful solutions not only to the issue at hand, but to the inner turmoil that prompted the outburst in the first place.

Meeting a child at their point of need when that need is expressed through meltdowns, yelling, disrespect, or defiance takes patience, self-control, and empathy on the part of a parent, which can be a huge growth experience for the parent if they, themselves, were not parented that way. But the impact of living those positive life skills in front of our children is immeasurable.

Parenting isn't a perfect science and parents aren't perfect people, but creating an overall atmosphere of respect in a home starts with the parents modeling respect in their own tone of voice, in their own reactions to stressful situations, in their own interactions with their children.

It's not easy, for sure. But the best things, the most valuable things, in life rarely are. Working toward being understanding, available, and responsive to our children's needs yields a priceless return in our relationship as the years fly by and adulthood looms. Not meeting those needs, though, may have serious negative consequences...

Dear Daughter,

> *You entered your teen years with a bang a few years ago, and the explosions have been shattering our home ever since. I've begged, threatened, bribed, and punished; cried, shouted, and bargained; but I just can't find a way to reach you anymore. You constantly say I don't listen to you, but how can I when you won't talk to me? You say I don't understand you, but how can I when you push me away? You say we aren't a family, but then spend every day with earphones in your ears, blocking us out. You ask me why I hate you, then roll your eyes when I tell you I love you.*

*How did it come to this? We used to be such a
happy family. Please, let me be there for you
during this huge transition in your life. Let's
really try to communicate with each other. I'm
just lost here, honey, and I need you to reach
out and help me reconnect with you. I love
you.*

Your Dad

'Dear' Dad,

*Happy family? Are you kidding me? No, I guess not.
You never did get it. Okay, you asked, so I'll tell you.
You were always happy because you were always in
control. Want to know why I don't talk to you now?
Because you never listened when I was little. When I
was scared in my room at night and called you, you
either ignored me or threatened to spank me if I didn't
go to sleep. I'd lay there, crying so hard I'd almost
throw up, terrified of the sounds and shadows in my
room, but even more terrified of you. So, sorry, but I
don't buy that you're 'there for me' when it's only ever
been at your own convenience. When you were mad at
something I'd done and I tried to explain myself, you'd
call it backtalk and smack me in the mouth. So forgive
me if I don't really believe you when you say you want
to 'communicate' with me now. When I'd try to show
you a dance I'd made up or tell you about how
someone had pushed me on the playground, you
couldn't even be bothered to look away from your
stupid computer while I was talking, so if I'm wrapped
up in my electronics, I learned that little trick from you,
Father Dear. Oh, and reconnect? Really? That implies
that we were once connected. But when I was a little
girl and invited you into my world and asked you to
play with me, you were always too busy. So if you don't
understand me, sorry, but that invitation expired years
ago. Want to know why I think you hate me? Because
your actions told me so. Your 'love' is just words.*

'Your' Daughter

Not all children react this way to harsh, punitive, control-based parenting, of course. Some children, due to personality, other influences and mentors in their lives, or simply as a survival instinct, will turn out okay despite how they are parented.

But 'okay' is too mediocre a goal when it comes to growing our children into the adults who will one day lead our world. Instead of raising children who turn out okay *despite* their childhood, let's raise children who turn out extraordinary *because of* their childhood. Let's grow excellent, outstanding, remarkable adults who will be world changers for the next generation and the generations to come. (*Whispers Through Time: Communication Through the Ages and Stages of Childhood*)

"You heard my cry for mercy when I called to you for help"
Psalm 31:22

Chapter 26

The Slingshot Effect

"Truly I tell you, unless you change and become like little children, you will never enter the kingdom of heaven."
Matthew 18:3

> *"Children are naturally inclined toward rebellion, selfishness, dishonesty, aggression, exploitation, and greed."[39] (Dr. James Dobson, The New Strong-Willed Child, p.45)*

Dobson is right. He is also incredibly wrong. Yes, children are naturally inclined toward all those things, and more, and so are we, the parents. The flip side of that coin, though, is that we all, parents and children and every other human, are also naturally inclined toward cooperation, sacrifice, honesty, peace, honor, and generosity.

We are, every one of us, inclined toward the full range of human behaviors and emotions, both positive and negative. We were created that way, and everything God creates is good. Yes, you read that right. We are *good*. But we can *do* bad. That is human nature. That is free will. And that is beautiful, messy, wonder-filled, chaotic, lovely, noisy, joyful, heartbreaking life here on earth.

It is *life*.

And it is *good*.

All of it.

Even the bad stuff.

Here's the thing, parents, we desire the best for our children, right? We don't want them to get hurt, but when they're learning to walk we don't tie them down to keep them from falling. We guide and guard them, of course, but inevitably in the learning process there are times they topple and bump a little head and then we scoop them up and kiss their tiny noggin before they're off to try again.

We don't want them to get scrapes and bruises, but we still let them learn to ride a bicycle and climb trees even though there are always times the learning process involves some tumbles and tears and we have to pick them up and wipe their tears before they're off to give it another shot.

We don't want them to be disappointed, but we don't discourage them from trying out for the football team or running for Student Council President or trying to win first prize at the science fair, even though there are inevitably times when they will fail and their hearts will be broken and we'll comfort and counsel them and then cheer them on as they try again.

The point is that even though we want the best for our children and want to keep them safe and happy, we accept that life comes with bumps and bruises and disappointments and we know that often the most valuable lessons are learned from failures instead of triumphs.

But when it comes to exploring all of the ins and outs and ups and downs of their own humanity, we often clamp down on them and try to control their behavior and even their emotions. When it comes to behavior and attitude, failure is met with punishment instead of guidance. So, instead of the same process of learning and discovering with the support of our wisdom, comfort, and counsel, they are constrained, contained, and restrained throughout childhood, effectively 'tied down' often through punishment, threats, and manipulations.

But what happens when childhood nears its end and those ties that bind are stretched to the breaking point by the indomitable human spirit of free will and independence? What can we do if our micro-control throughout our children's early years leads to macro-rebellion in the latter stages of childhood? What are our options if our early parenting was controlling and graceless and the slingshot effect has launched our teen so far in the opposite direction that there seems to be no way back?

It's not easy to repair what's been broken, to recapture what's been lost, but there are steps we can take to bring healing and restoration to our relationship with our hurting teens:

When children aren't parented in the early years with gentleness and respect, the teen years can hit the family with the force of a hurricane. Parents who have felt confident in their control over their children up until this point often find themselves lost, dazed, and bewildered, entangled in a parenting morass of their own making. The truths they discover shock them and leave them vulnerable and defenseless in the face of outright or passive mutiny:

1. *Hitting doesn't lead to hugging.* Just ask the mother struggling with her teenage daughter who had become withdrawn around the age of twelve or thirteen, often spending hours in her room and refusing to engage with the rest of the family. The mother recognized that there was a problem, but interpreted it as laziness, selfishness, and rebellion. The mother said, "She won't accept discipline given in love anymore, and I don't know how to control her behavior." The 'discipline given in love' was being spanked with a paddle wielded by a parent who then demanded an apology from the child for her behavior, followed by a hug. This mother was discovering that, once her daughter reached her teen years, she no longer accepted the hitting, and she no longer accepted the hugs, either.

2. Lectures don't lead to learning. Just ask the father who complained that every time he sat his son down to read him the riot act for something, he could see his son's eyes glaze over as the teen retreated to an inner world. The father would

repeatedly demand that his son pay attention, and his son would then quote his lecture verbatim, but nothing worked to change his son's behavior. The father shared, "I don't know what to do. How can I control my son if I can't reach him?" What this father is discovering is that lecturing instead of listening is a one-way street that leads nowhere.

3. Coercion doesn't lead to cooperation. Just ask the mother who was so frustrated with her son's inability to finish his math homework that she began to take his things and hold them as ransom to try to force him to cooperate. She emptied his room piece by piece, day after day, until she'd literally taken away everything he owned, including every article of clothing except for the clothes on his back. After six weeks of her son wearing the same clothes and sleeping on the floor, she said, "I don't know what else I can take away from him. He doesn't have anything left! How can I control him now?" What this mother found was that you can't force cooperation and children outgrow coercion just like they outgrow clothing.

4. Ridicule doesn't lead to respect. Just ask the father who made his daughter post on Facebook that she had lied to her parents about her screen-time and couldn't be trusted to have a laptop, so she wouldn't be online for a month. The father was infuriated to then discover that his daughter was using friends' computers, so he made her call every one of her friends' parents and explain why she wouldn't be visiting for the next month. When the father found out his daughter was using the computers at the public library, he made her stand in front of the library with a sign that said, "I'm a liar." A week later the father found his daughter in her room online in the middle of the night, using a laptop borrowed from a friend. The father said, "What can I do? Every time I find a way to control

my daughter, she finds a way around it. How can I make her respect me?" What this father is finding is that you can't force respect. Ridicule and shame are disrespectful and only breed more disrespect.

What these parents are discovering, and what you may have already discovered yourself as your children have reached adolescence, is that no matter how much you escalate punishments, they won't work to get your children under *your* control because one human can never really control another. Yes, you can overpower a small child, and you can use fear and intimidation and manipulation to force children to comply, but only for a season. Once they reach the teen years and their own identity begins to fully emerge, they gain enough separation to realize that they can finally say no to the hitting and threats and manipulations. They may say no with outright rebellion or by withdrawing into passive resistance, but they *will* say no, and then you are lost because you haven't built a relationship based on mutual respect and cooperation. You've simply spent years forcing your will on a smaller, weaker human.

Can you make changes, even this late in parenting? Yes. Stop hitting, threatening, intimidating, coercing, shaming, and trying to control your child. Wipe the slate clean with a sincere apology, and then start rebuilding your relationship from the ground up:

- Create a foundation of trust by proving *yourself* trustworthy. That means honoring your word that you won't punish or manipulate your teen to try to control them, no matter what.

- Sacrifice your own hopes and dreams for your teen and support *their* hopes and dreams. Will they make mistakes? Yes. That's part of life. Let them make the mistakes without repercussion from you, and help them through the natural results of those mistakes so they will know they can count on you when life hurts.

- Set limits *with* your teen instead of *for* your teen. Ask their opinion about curfews and relationships and housework. Tell them that it's an honor system from this point on, no punishments, and ask them how you can help them to honor the limits they've helped set.

- Remember that, while your teen is rapidly approaching adulthood, they are still a child and still need guidance. Don't disconnect (i.e. give up) and just let your teen figure things out for themselves. Yes, they do need to try and fail and try again so they can learn from their mistakes, but that doesn't mean they don't need you. Your role at this point is supportive as you stay in-tune and available and help them to process all of the big transitions and emotions and events that happen in adolescence. Walk them through the problem-solving steps of identifying the problem, brainstorming solutions, selecting and implementing solutions, evaluating progress, etc. as many times as they need you to so that they can learn how to become problem-solvers themselves.

- If they backtalk, LISTEN (see Chapter Twenty-Five). If they struggle with homework, help them. If they lie, forgive them and work with them to come to a place where they feel safe to be truthful. If they break curfew, ask them why and work with them to sort out the problem.

- Memorize these words, "I'm here. I hear you. How can I help?" They encapsulate the Three C's of gentle parenting—Connection. Communication. Cooperation. Use them every day to rebuild your relationship.

The thing to remember is that you are the only adult in the relationship for the time being, so be the first one to listen, the first one to forgive, the first one to apologize, the first one to understand, the first one to back down and try to find another way when the going gets tough. Before you know it, your teen will be an adult, just like you… Just. Like. You. Make sure the 'you' they see is the 'you' that you want them to become. (*The Gentle Parent: Positive, Practical, Effective Discipline*)

"Love is patient, love is kind. It does not envy, it does not boast, it is not proud. It does not dishonor others, it is not self-seeking, it is not easily angered, it keeps no record of wrongs. Love does not delight in evil but rejoices with the truth. It always protects, always trusts, always hopes, always perseveres."
1 Corinthians 13:4-8

Chapter 27

Not Sweetly Broken...Fiercely LIVING!

"Let us then approach God's throne of grace with confidence,
so that we may receive mercy and find grace to help us
in our time of need."
Hebrews 4:16

The Old Testament is a tragic tale of humans who have lost their
way home and with desperate futility are trying to work their
way back to God.

The Cross is a tragically beautiful truth that we don't have to...

We don't have to try to reach God. We don't have to struggle to
please him. We don't have to fix ourselves up and wash
ourselves down to make ourselves acceptable. The work is
finished. It was finished on the Cross. We are God's children,
and we are wholly and fully and *unconditionally* loved.

"See what kind of love the Father has given to us, that we should
be called children of God; and so we are." (1 John 3:1)

"But God demonstrates his own love for us in this: While we
were still sinners, Christ died for us." (Romans 5:8)

"Can a mother forget the baby at her breast and have no
compassion on the child she has borne? Though she may forget,
I will not forget you! See, I have engraved you on the palms of
my hands" (Isaiah 49:15-16)

"There is no fear in love. But perfect love drives out fear,
because fear has to do with punishment. The one who fears is
not made perfect in love." (1 John 4:18)

Here's the thing, we *can't* be perfect, and that is why we are
afraid. We are afraid that we aren't loved, aren't acceptable. We
feel unworthy and unlovable. We think we need to be punished

to be made acceptable, and, by the same token, that is why we believe our children need to be punished, to make them obedient and acceptable.

But did you catch that last verse? It says, "*made perfect in love*," not "*be* perfect *to be* loved." We are made perfect *in* love. That means God, Love Himself, has made us acceptable *because* he loves us, not so that he *can* love us.

God tells us to "*approach the throne of grace with confidence*," not with a confidence born of good behavior or good obedience or good deeds, but born of trust in a good and perfect Father. He doesn't say, "when you're good enough" or "when you've got it all figured out" or "when *you*...anything."

He says come, "*in your time of need*." When you're battered and bloody and bruised by life and your own mistakes, you are welcome...no, you are *invited* to come running to your Father who waits with open arms and to climb into his lap and be wrapped in the comfort and healing of his embrace.

That is the heart of a Father. That is God's heart for his children. And that is the heart our children need to see in us and hear from us and learn from their relationship with us.

Using fear, threats, intimidation, and manipulation to train our children into obedience misses the heart of God entirely and effectively places "a millstone around their necks" as we layer shame and guilt on them.

Until we can grasp the stunning, miraculous truth that we, *ourselves*, are free, truly free, from punishment (i.e. separation from God) and are welcome to run to the throne and climb in God's lap even when we're battered and bloody and bruised from our own bad choices, then we will always struggle with our own faith and trust and we will continue to hold our children accountable (punishing them to make them 'pay the price' for their choices; using punishment and threats to try to drive them to good behavior) instead of washing them with the grace we've been given (offering acceptance and wisdom to invite them to mutual respect and cooperation).

True obedience (in the original text of the Bible *hupakouo/ hupakoe, shema/lishmoa* - thoughtfully consider, lend an ear to)[1,2,3] is an alignment of our hearts with God's heart, not an adherence to a series of do's and don'ts. The do's and don'ts in the Bible (i.e. commands, instructions, guidance, wisdom, etc.) are for our happiness, well-being, and safety. They aren't a way to earn God's approval or acceptance. We already have those. They aren't given to constrain and restrain us from living life joyfully and abundantly. They are given so that we *can* live life joyfully and abundantly.

"I came that they may have life, and have it abundantly." (John 10:10)

"Every good thing given and every perfect gift is from above, coming down from the Father of lights, with whom there is no variation or shifting shadow." (James 1:17)

We sing about being sweetly broken, but we forget that God invites us to live fully and freely, to enjoy his good and perfect gifts. We focus on the suffering of the Cross, on "taking up our Cross to follow him," but we lose sight of the *freedom* given on the Cross. But when we empty the greatest gift ever given of its goodness, we are left with a hollow shell, a shadow of the extravagant and deep and lavishly rich relationship God wants to have with his children.

Consider…

> *A father works tirelessly to provide for his children. His backbreaking labor begins before dawn each day, but as he toils in the blistering sun his heart is light and his eyes dance for joy because he knows he is working for his children. One day, he comes home and bursts in the door, excitement lighting his face as he hands each of his children a ticket to Disney World that he's scraped and saved and worked overtime to purchase. They all squeal with delight and throw their arms around their daddy in grateful hugs.*

*The next day, the father packs his children in the car
and heads to Disney, everyone singing and cheering on
the journey. But when they arrive, the children refuse to
ride the rides. They won't eat the ice cream or watch
the parades or oooh and aaah over the fireworks. They
will only walk in single file, carefully avoiding the
puddles and confetti and litter left over from other
people's fun. Occasionally they see someone trying to
find their way and the children stop and offer
directions, but then they resume their staid walk down
the streets of the most magical place on earth.*

*Throughout the day, the father points out the laughing
children on the rides and offers his children ice cream
and invites his children to enjoy the parades and
fireworks with him, but to no avail. When they arrive
home, the disheartened father asks his children if they
enjoyed the day. They proudly shake their heads and
say, "No. We wanted to honor you, so we were careful
not to get dirty or muddy. We didn't make noise or mess
up our clothes, either, daddy. And we helped to guide
the lost. Aren't you happy with us?"*

*The father sighs and draws his children close to his
heart, "I was already happy with you, little ones. I just
wanted to see your smiles and hear your laughter ring
out in the sunshine. I wanted to wipe your ice-cream-
sticky faces and see your eyes light up with delight at
the dazzling displays of light and life. Don't you know I
love you just the way you are, my children? You don't
have to try to please me. I don't love you because of
what you do. I love you because of who you are."*

Remember, parents, *we* are our children's first taste of God, and
his wondrous, miraculous delight in his children's delight is an
integral part of who he is and how he relates to us. Let's be
reflectors of his goodness and love, conveyors of his acceptance
and forgiveness, conduits for his grace and mercy. Let's connect,
communicate, and cooperate with our children to guide them

gently, compassionately, and peacefully in the short season they are in our homes so that they will carry that gentleness, compassion, and peace into the world as reflectors of the heart of our Father.

"Taste and see that the Lord is good"
Psalm 34:8

Chapter 28

Running From the Morality Police

*"If anyone hears my words but does not keep them,
I do not judge that person. For I did not come to judge the
world, but to save the world."*
John 12:47

Often in the teen years parents shift their focus and begin to
obsess about morality with their children, hoping to stave off
bad adolescent choices by emphasizing the "wages of sin." They
lecture about sex and drugs and rebellion incessantly, running in
mental circles in a fear-crazed fog. While it's understandable
and even commendable to set high standards and to teach our
children our values and morals, an all-out war against sin, or
potential sin, can backfire in a number of ways.

First, focusing on sin puts the focus in the wrong place. Just like
when we're driving and our eyes stray from the road and we find
ourselves drifting in the direction of our gaze, we tend to head in
the direction our thoughts and focus take us.

A grace-focus, by contrast, directs our thoughts and actions with
our children, helping us to focus on maintaining our connection
and relationship and keeping our teens grounded by the giving
and receiving of grace.

What that looks like on a daily basis is *acceptance*. Teens who
know they will be heard don't have to fight to be heard. Teens
who know they will be trusted understand the value of that trust
and will work to maintain it. Teens who are forgiven when they
inevitably make a mistake, as all humans do, will value that
forgiveness and learn to share that forgiveness with others
(including their all-too-human parents).

Second, focusing on sin puts the emphasis on the consequences
of sin instead of on the Cross. It makes avoiding sin the point
instead of seeking the Cross the point. But humans don't have a
great track record of avoiding sin. In fact, sin is inevitable as
long as we are here in our present state. If that weren't true, then
perfection would be possible and the Cross would be pointless:

> *"I do not set aside the grace of God, for if*
> *righteousness could be gained through the law,*
> *Christ died for nothing!" (Galatians 2:21)*

Grace-focused parenting creates a safe environment to grow and learn and explore, to make mistakes and learn from those mistakes. And, with every forgiven mistake, with every outpouring of grace, the Cross grows ever nearer and dearer to their hearts.

What this looks like on a daily basis is *approval*. When teens know that they are not just loved, but really and truly liked, when they know that it isn't what they do or don't do that wins our approval, but simply who they are, then they are free to try and fail and live and learn with the sure knowledge that they have a safe place to come home to, no matter what.

Third, focusing on sin can create an adversarial relationship with our teens just when we need to work with them closely through the ofttimes turbulent ups and downs of the adolescent years. It can create barriers to communication, worries about acceptance, and impediments to healthy independence. It can place us in the hypocritical position of one sinner holding another sinner accountable and make us seem distant and unreachable, and the result can be teens who are distant and unteachable.

Parenting with a grace-focus brings us together as a united team with our teens, connects us, and opens those all-important lines of communication when they are most needed.

What this looks like on a daily basis is *availability*. When teens know that we are there for them, day or night, in good times and in bad, through their good choices and their not-so-good choices, then they are free to explore all of the possibilities and potential that life has to offer, to challenge themselves and overcome obstacles, to grow and develop into the miraculous humans God created them to be without fear of having to navigate the inevitable bumps and bruises and wrong turns along the way alone.

The bottom line is, focusing on sin is pointless because sin is a moot point. Grace is and always will be the point...the *only* point. And, interestingly enough, when avoiding sin is not the focus, its hold loosens on all of us, teens included, freeing us even more to embrace the power of the Cross and to joyfully live in and lavishly give out grace.

Walking out acceptance, approval, and availability with our teens can be a challenge, of course, especially if we weren't parented that way, ourselves. But it's never too late to begin building the trust relationship that underpins grace-based parenting, just as it's never too late for us to receive grace from and walk in accord with our Father.

Here are some tips to help you on your gentle journey with your terrific teens:

Talking with your Teens

> Communication is always a huge concern for parents of adolescents. The strong, open communication channel created and mutual respect and trust foundation established in the early years through gentle parenting provide a powerful platform for a healthy parent/teen relationship. Simply put, children and teens who feel heard and understood and respected don't need to fight to be heard, understood, and respected. Or, conversely, they don't slip away into the sullen, angry, withdrawn teen who doesn't bother to even try to be heard anymore because they never felt heard or understood as a young child.

> Again, this is not to say that the gently raised adolescent will be perfect. None of us are! But with a healthy relationship based on open, honest communication, issues can be addressed as they arise and in a respectful and timely manner instead of a teen feeling the need to go 'underground' with their behavior or problems.

> So, that said, what are some practical tips for talking to teens?

> 1. *Honesty is paramount.* Teens will tune out faster than you can imagine if they sense

you're being less than transparent with them. Only in a mutually honest environment will a teen be willing to share their deepest fears, hopes, disappointments, etc.

2. *Judgment-free zone.* Along with this goes the need to be able to say anything, anything at all, and know that they will be heard and accepted without judgment, without repercussion. Consequences for broken rules should never come as a result of a heart-to-heart discussion, or it may well be the last heart-to-heart your teen will have with you. You can and should honestly express your concern and even disappointment if appropriate, but don't make it all about yourself or the conversation and chance for real connection will end.

3. *Respect is key.* Embarrassment is like Kryptonite to a teen. Ridiculing them, making light of their feelings, minimizing their experiences by 'one-upping' them with yours are surefire ways to shut down a conversation with a teen permanently.

4. *Reassurance is healing.* Teens need to know they are normal. They need to hear that everyone has 'bad' thoughts sometimes and that doesn't make them a 'bad person.' Sharing some crazy thoughts that have popped into your head through the years and how "It's not the thought, it's what you do with the thought that matters" will help them to realize that they aren't abnormal. (You'd be surprised how many teens think they're abnormal. 'Normal' matters to them HUGELY.)

5. *Burn the midnight oil.* Adolescents seem to be naturally nocturnal creatures. When the house is quiet and nothing is competing for attention, guards begin to drop, emotions mellow, and in

the stillness of the night, soft-voiced conversations invite deep, meaningful discussions. Don't let the busyness and business of life rob you of these sweet moments with your teens who will so very soon be off on their own in the adult world.

Dealing with the Hard Stuff

Addressing difficult life issues with teens is not something most parents look forward to, particularly, and often flat out dread. Some parents just don't address these issues, period, often with excuses such as, *"They need to find out what they believe for themselves."*

But simply avoiding talking about difficult issues doesn't make them go away, and often teens left to fend for themselves become overwhelmed with societal pressures, an endless array of choices, and conflicting information. Leaving them to *"figure out what they believe themselves"* just leaves them without the guidance and wisdom they need from those they trust the most and may lead to feelings of resentment and abandonment as well as to poor choices.

It can, of course, be challenging to address hard issues like sex, morality, war, politics, religion, etc. with your teen. Teenagers do a fantastic imitation of bloodhounds. Hypocrisy, fear, 'smudging' the truth, you name it, they can sniff it out in a heartbeat. When talking about these difficult life issues, it's far better to be transparent about any doubts or failings or confusion you may have because your teen will know if you try to gloss it over.

Got some skeletons in your closet? Dust them off and pull them out as object lessons and connection points. Your teen will learn more from one confession (no need to go into graphic detail) than from a hundred lectures.

Ambivalent about current events? Discuss the inner conflict you're having.

Passionate about your spiritual beliefs? Tell them how that feels and what brought you to that point.

Sharing your heart, your experiences, your struggles, honestly and often, with your teen will make an impact on them that no amount of bookwork or lecturing or training can possibly match. Keep in mind, too, that this is a life conversation and not just confined to adolescence. Beginning this kind of sharing early in your child's life in age-appropriate ways establishes the vital communication channel that is central to gentle parenting, and keeping the conversation open-ended helps to maintain healthy familial ties with your children even when they're adults, themselves. Remember, we never outgrow the human need for connection.

Too Late for Teens?

So what do you do if you're the parent of a teenager and have only just discovered gentle parenting? Is it too late to implement any of the gentle parenting philosophy, to establish connectedness and mutual respect, and to ease the transition into adulthood? And what if your teenager is in full-on rebellion mode? Is there anything gentle parenting can do for you?

The answers aren't easy, by any means. Making changes at this stage is as challenging as teens themselves can be. But, that said, there are some basic tenets that you can begin the hard work of weaving into your parenting even at this late stage:

1. *Don't engage in arguments.* Win or lose, they'll enjoy the argument, and you won't. Teens often simply enjoy a good debate, while adults just end up more frustrated.

2. *Apologize.* Take responsibility for past and present parenting mistakes. As mentioned earlier, teens can sniff out hypocrisy like bloodhounds, and acting like you're perfect (which is how they'll interpret that missing apology) smells an awful lot like hypocrisy to them.

3. *Be real.* Nothing will make a teen more resentful than you demanding behavior from them that you aren't modeling in your own life.

4. *Be available.* If you haven't been available in the past, openly let your teen know that you've made mistakes and would like to change, then let them know you are available to them, day or night, whether your favorite tv show is on or not, even if you have work to do, or emails to read, or phone calls to return...no matter what. Don't be surprised if they test you on this. Even adults tend to test out changes before we fully believe we can count on them.

5. *Communicate.* If you feel your early parenting hasn't established the open communication vital to a healthy parent/teen relationship, it isn't too late to make some renovations to bridge the gap. Just start talking...about your own life, your own struggles, your own needs, and just start sharing, about your love for them, your hopes for them, your pride in them. And start asking questions, not prying, but providing an opening for them to talk about their lives. If they aren't ready to open up yet, don't push. Just be there, ready to listen when they're ready to talk.

6. *Let go.* When a child reaches the teen years, it's time to begin slowly releasing them from parental controls and start letting them make more of their own choices. This is not to say that you stop being their parent, but that you begin to consciously shift your role in your teen's life further and further away from guardian and caretaker, and closer and closer to a supportive, accepting, mentoring role…in short, a friendship role that will set the stage for your relationship with your adult child. This conscious shifting on your part will help to make your teen's transition from child to adult a cooperative effort between you rather than a source of conflict.

7. *Move.* If your teen is involved with a bad group, is immersed in drugs, gangs, etc…pack up and move. I know it's easier said than done. I know there are all kinds of job and economic issues involved. I know it's a huge sacrifice. And I know they'll fight you on it. But if everything else has failed, removing them from negative influences and situations to give them a chance at a fresh start may be the best, or only, choice. And, letting your teen know that they are the first and most important priority in your life, more important than your job, home, the life you've built, or anything else, will in and of itself go a long way toward healing your relationship. *Note: Blaming your teen for the move, inwardly or outwardly, will undermine your reasons for moving. Make peace in your own heart with the move ahead of time so you'll be up to the challenges inherent in all big life changes. (*Two Thousand Kisses a Day: Gentle Parenting Through the Ages and Stages*)

"For it is by grace you have been saved, through faith--and this is not from yourselves, it is the gift of God"
Ephesians 2:8

Chapter 29

The Still, Small Voice

*"...a great and strong wind tore into the mountains and
broke the rocks in pieces before the Lord, but the Lord was not
in the wind; and after the wind an earthquake, but the Lord was
not in the earthquake; and after the earthquake a fire, but
the Lord was not in the fire; and after the fire
a still small voice..."
1 Kings 19:11-12*

When you read God's Word, what do you hear? Do you hear the
voice of an angry, overbearing, condemning Father demanding
instant and unquestioning obedience? Do you hear the voice of
an intimidating, domineering, distant Father issuing threats and
calling down curses on your head?

So often when we read God's Word we hear what we've heard
from the pulpit instead of hearing the voice of a Father who
loves unconditionally, sacrificially, and eternally. And so often
what we've heard from the pulpit is accusation, damnation, and
condemnation. It's no wonder we have problems trusting in
God's unconditional love if all we hear are commands, demands,
and reprimands echoed in those misguided voices.

I recently read a story about someone who asked God to move a
mountain and was answered with a prompt, "Yes!" and a
shovel.[42] (Esther, Girl at the End of the World) That's what it
can feel like when you're digging and sifting and winnowing
your way through years of hearing human interpretations of
God's Word spoken from the pulpit and from Sunday school
teachers and Bible camp counselors and parents and friends and
relatives, etc.

Working our way through all of the human ideas about what
God says and who God is and what he wants and how he relates
to us to a place where we find God's heart and can actually hear
God's voice ourselves and get to know him personally and feel
him moving and guiding and loving us is a hugely challenging,

intensely moving, constantly evolving, and incredibly enlightening journey.

Humans aren't perfect and, no matter how wise, how conscientious, how educated they are, the simple fact is that the human mind cannot fully grasp the mind and heart of God and, therefore, their interpretations of the Bible must always be regarded with careful examination instead of absolute faith.

The thing is, though, that we *can* find God's heart. We have direct access. God's heart came to earth as a baby, lived and loved and laughed with God's precious children, and then was hung on a Cross, died, and was resurrected, defeating death for God's children once and for all.

But after years and years of hearing humans tell us what God said and what he meant in his Word, it can be incredibly hard to discern God's voice for ourselves. Let's take a look at some verses and listen carefully for the "the still, small voice" that whispers from the heart of love...

> *"Do not be anxious about anything, but in every situation, by prayer and petition, with thanksgiving, present your requests to God. And the peace of God, which transcends all understanding, will guard your hearts and your minds in Christ Jesus." (Philippians 4:6-7)*

> Listen for the still, small voice...comforting, not controlling:

> *"Don't worry, little one. I'm right here. Come to me with what you need. I'll help."*

> Can you hear the voice of comfort?

"'Love the Lord your God with all your heart and with all your soul and with all your strength and with all your mind' and, 'Love your neighbor as yourself'..."Do this and you will live." (Luke 10:27 & 28)

Listen for the still, small voice...tender, not tyrannical:

"Love me as I have loved you, wholeheartedly, extravagantly, with everything you have and everything you are, and love my children the same way, fully accepting, graciously giving, because that is where you will find me and, in me, you will find life."

Can you hear the voice of tenderness?

"Be still, and know that I am God." (Psalm 46:10)

Listen for the still, small voice…reassuring, not reprimanding:

"I've got this, so you can relax and trust me, little one."

Can you hear the voice of reassurance?

"Be dressed in readiness, and keep your lamps lit." (Luke 12:35)

Listen for the still, small voice…wise, not wrathful:

"Don't worry, little ones, put on the safe covering of Jesus and keep your love and your hope alive."

Can you hear the voice of wisdom?

"The Lord's bond-servant must not be quarrelsome, but be kind to all, able to teach, patient when wronged." (2 Timothy 2:24)

Listen for the still, small voice…counseling, not commanding:

"You're attached to me at the heart, my children, so let your heart reflect my peace, my kindness, my teaching, my forgiveness."

Can you hear the voice of counsel?

As travelers looked to the stars in ancient times to guide them on their journeys, so we look to God as our guiding light. The Hebrew word *halal* means to 'look toward another as a shining light,'[1,2,3] so when the psalmist says, '*Praise Yah (halelu-Yah)*' it literally means to "Look to Yah (the Lord) as the light that will guide you on your journey."

And so listen, parents, for the still, small voice of love, wisdom, and guidance from God, the *only* source of truth. The viewpoints, analysis, and interpretations of scripture that you've read here in *Jesus, the Gentle Parent*, like all others, must be examined, discussed, and prayed over instead of taken on faith. Keep your faith for God alone. When you read the words in this book, don't accept them. Question them. Challenge them. Test them. Pray about them. Ask God to give you eyes to see and ears to hear so that you can make your own decisions based on God's wise and wonderful counsel.

"But blessed are your eyes, because they see; and your ears, because they hear. For truly I say to you that many prophets and righteous men desired to see what you see, and did not see it, and to hear what you hear, and did not hear it."
Matthew 13:16-17

APPENDIX A

Seasons of Love

"If I speak in the tongues of men and of angels,
but have not love, I am a noisy gong or a clanging cymbal.
And if I have prophetic powers, and understand all mysteries
and all knowledge, and if I have all faith, so as to remove
mountains, but have not love, I am nothing. If I give away all
I have, and if I deliver up my body to be burned, but have not
love, I gain nothing. Love is patient and kind; love does not envy
or boast; it is not arrogant or rude. It does not insist on its own
way; it is not irritable or resentful; it does not rejoice at
wrongdoing, but rejoices with the truth.
Love bears all things, believes all things,
hopes all things, endures all things.
Love never ends."
1 Corinthians 13:1-8

Whether you are reading this book as a new Christian or a veteran believer, a young parent or a seasoned grandparent, an eager learner or a hardened sceptic, I hope that you will come away with a deeper, clearer understanding of what you believe and why you believe it. Whether you agree with everything you've read here, some of what you've read here, or none of what you've read here, I pray that you at least have had the opportunity to pause and ponder and pray about what you believe and why you believe it.

We are all here on earth to learn and grow and experience and discover, and each of us are at our own unique stage in our own unique journey. From the vantage point of each age and stage, love and life and faith can look very different, and that is perfectly okay...

An aged beauty tips her face up, and her elderly
companion leans down out of life-long habit to catch

her soft voice. His old eyes see past the ever-deepening lines to the vision of youth he married decades earlier. His hands reach out to steady her fragile, but oh-so-familiar frame, and she smiles the same smile he's woken up to and kissed goodnight his entire adult life. Theirs is an old love, subtle with wear, ripe with age, its rich beauty lost to those without the palate to plumb its boundless depths or the senses to delight in its warm bouquet. They are a living love story, two hearts time-stitched into one, beautiful old souls stepping in tandem toward eternity.

Truly, love does have many seasons and faces, each revealing its own power, its own purpose...

Young love shouts from the rooftops and expresses itself in passionate displays. Its flames are brilliant, stoked with newness and fueled with idealism, but at times it burns itself out with its own heat or through lack of care and tending.

Old love whispers quietly, *"I'm here. No matter what, I'm always here."* It is a silent glance, a hand clasp, a timeless commitment.

Young love, blind to the rich time-tested tapestry, deaf to the wealth of meaning in quiet companionship, lost to the supple oneness of hearts in accord, often looks at old love and calls it dead.

Old love sometimes looks at young love and smiles with fond remembrance, but ofttimes shakes its head and declares it foolish.

Each has a place in the world, a purpose, a time, and a season.

And then there are the other faces of love...

The exhausted young mother tenderly cradling a brand new life in the early morning hours. The middle-aged man getting up at four o'clock in the morning for another backbreaking day of work to support his family. The teacher spending her meager pay to make sure her students have pencils. The pastor visiting a convicted felon just to play a game of cards. The teenager stopping to help a stranger push their stalled car to the side of the road...

Each speaks love in a different language, but the message is the same...love is alive.

There is another Love, a living, breathing, timeless, endless, lavish, inconceivable, unconditional, sacrificial, unlikely Love. His name is Love because he *is* Love. He and I have an old love, a stalwart and enduring love, a time-tested, unraveled and rewoven, wounded and healed, shattered and renewed love.

In the beginning, when I was newly in love with my Love, his passion fueled mine and I was consumed. I flared white-hot and brandished his Name like a sword, intent on conquering the world all on my own and presenting it as a treasure to my Love. I scorned the quiet love of my elders as a burned-out relic, not fit for my King.

Then time passed and life happened. My Love clung to me fiercely through the storms, even as my own grasp weakened and slipped. My Love held me close in the dark and never let go even when I kicked and flailed and railed at him because I couldn't see him through my tears.

And, over time, my young love grew into an old love, deep and rich and still. Our old love is a stunning tapestry of life and loss, triumph and tragedy, joy and heartache, woven from the tattered and torn remnants of our young love.

Now, in place of conquering the world, I let him love the world through me. Instead of proselytizing, evangelizing, and sermonizing for my King, I let his love permeate all I do like the subtle fragrance of rain as it washes clean the earth. Rather than feverishly working to present My Love a treasure, I bask in his presence knowing I *am* his treasure.

And our beautiful old souls step lightly toward eternity...

As we grow and change, our perspective will naturally grow and change with us. My hope is that some of what you've read here will help to light your way as you seek to grow and guide the beautiful little souls entrusted to your care.

"Now I know in part; then I shall know fully, even as I have been fully known. So now faith, hope, and love abide, these three; but the greatest of these is love."
1 Corinthians 13:12-13

APPENDIX B

The Way of the Parable

"We speak the wisdom of God in a mystery, even the hidden wisdom which God ordained before the world to our glory"
1 Corinthians 2:7

Did you ever wonder why Jesus chose the way of the parable when relating deep truths to his disciples and followers? Wouldn't it have been easier to simply say, "Every one of my children is precious to me," instead of telling the Parable of the Lost Sheep? Or, "It is your kindness and compassion to my children that show true love for me, not your meetings and buildings and busyness," instead of sharing the story of the Good Samaritan?

Easier? Probably. But he knew what his children needed.

Consider...

St. Nicholas was just a man, but he was a man with a mission. Born in the third century, he grew up to be an intensely kind-hearted man who was especially devoted to children's issues and helping the poor. He was a Greek Bishop who defied the established Church in order to go out among the 'unwashed masses' and live his life as the 'heart and hands of Jesus.' While many legends about him evolved through the centuries, his penchant for leaving secret gifts is the one that captured the hearts and imaginations of people world-wide, leading to the present-day legend of Santa Claus.

I, like many new parents, struggled with the idea of perpetuating a 'false belief' and thus undermining my children's trust. But then I turned to the Bible and saw how Jesus, who spoke absolute truth always, often spoke that truth in stories. He knew something about people's hearts that I needed to learn as a young parent. He knew that the human mind is logic, analysis, reason, and that the human heart is imagination, creativity, love. He knew that sometimes you have to bypass people's minds and speak straight to their hearts, those well-springs of wonder, for true understanding to occur and that often the deepest truths are the ones that are too big for the human mind to receive and can only be grasped by the heart.

When it comes to the breathtaking gift of the Christ-Child, the Eternal Creator born of a woman, God Himself wrapped in swaddling clothes, the I AM in a manger, what better way to share such an absurd and immense truth than Jesus' way…with a story? How else would my little ones be able to grasp the concept of such a gift? How would they embrace the wonder?

How could I possibly break down the impossible into a pedantic lecture? Would the improbable make more sense in a dissertation?

And so I chose the way of the parable. I embraced Christmas in all its glory, decorated and baked and showered my little ones with gifts, all while sharing the story of the birth of a Baby. Woven through every event, every tradition, every memorable moment of our family's Christmas, is the celebration of the wondrous gift of a Savior. We watch *Rudolph the Red-Nosed Reindeer, Santa Claus is Coming to Town*, and all the other fun Christmas shows together. We read bedtime stories about Christmas elves and magical toys and talking animals. And when my children ask me if Santa really exists, I tell them yes, because it's true. Every parent who carries on St. Nicholas' tradition of leaving secret gifts, of being the heart and hands of Jesus, of sharing the wonder, excitement, and glory of the most extraordinary Gift ever given to mankind, every one of us is Santa Claus.

I believe in Santa Claus because I am Santa Claus…and that is exactly what I tell my children when they are old enough to ask if Santa is real. I say, "Yes, Santa Claus was a real man named St. Nicholas who loved children and wanted to make them happy. Just as we are the heart and hands of Jesus, who was and is as real as you and I are, we can also share the joy of Christmas by giving gifts to celebrate the greatest Gift ever given just like St. Nicholas did for children many years ago. Every time we give a gift on Christmas, we are Santa Claus."

On a side note, I don't ever use Santa Claus as a threat (i.e. *"I'm calling Santa right now if you don't..."* or *"Santa's watching, and you won't get any presents for Christmas if..."*) first because a parable's purpose is to teach, not to manipulate or control, and second because what I am teaching is the wonder and miracle of receiving a free gift, one that can't be earned because it is freely given. Manipulating my children into 'performing' might work temporarily, but am I really trying to raise works-driven Christians, or am I trying to teach my little people about the incredible gift of grace?

Here are some of the ways we focus on Jesus for Christmas:

- Children learn best and most happily through play, imagination, and creativity, so letting my little people play Santa by wrapping up their toys and 'surprising' each other, making ornaments and delivering them to a local nursing home, and shopping at the dollar store for gifts for Christmas shoeboxes to be shipped to children in need is a very important part of our Christmas traditions.

- Leading up to Christmas, we marvel about how Jesus loves us so much he wants us to get presents on his birthday (truly awe-inspiring to children and a lesson in sacrificial giving!) because all he wants for his birthday is to see their smiles and happy hearts.

- We brainstorm ways to give Jesus as many 'birthday presents' as possible (a lesson on generosity). We work together to share Christmas cheer with everyone we meet, but focus our best efforts on the grumpiest people because they don't smile as often and so their smiles make really special gifts for Jesus (a lesson on unconditional love!).

- We have a 12 Days of Christmas tradition in which everyone gets a small present and we read Christmas picture books every evening, building excitement for the Christmas morning celebration of the BEST GIFT EVER!

- On Christmas Eve, we go to a special church service and then, after celebrating Christmas with family, we go home and make a fire in the fireplace (in Florida weather!) and make s'mores and hot chocolate and read the story of Jesus' birth from the Gospel of Luke.

- On Christmas morning, we have a 'Happy Birthday, Jesus' party before opening presents, complete with a birthday cake and candles and singing 'Happy birthday to Jesus!

Flights of fantasy, wonder, and awe are vehicles through which all of us, not only children, can grasp the inexplicable, understand the unimaginable, embrace the extraordinary.

I want my children to dance with excitement as the Christmas season begins with the ringing sound of carols and the glitter of decorations filling our home. I want them to wonder and imagine as we read Christmas stories and watch Christmas classics together under warm blankets with bowls of buttery popcorn and piping hot mugs of hot cocoa. I want them to gasp in awe at the brilliant abundance of presents under the Christmas tree as we gather on Christmas morning and sing 'Happy Birthday to Jesus' before the tumble-bumble, joyful chaos of gift opening begins.

I want these things for them so that as they grow up they'll take these memories of joy and laughter and wonder and awe with them and always be able feel the beauty of the Gift we were given in the Christ Child instead of just having head knowledge of Him.

"For God so loved the world, that he gave his only Son, that whoever believes in him should not perish but have eternal life."
John 3:16

APPENDIX C

Twelve Steps to Gentle Parenting:
Setting Yourself Up for Success

*From *Two Thousand Kisses a Day: Gentle Parenting Through*
the Ages and Stages

It's been said that it takes twenty-one days to make or break a habit and that change comes easiest and lasts longest when it's undertaken in small, bite-sized chunks. Those same principles apply when trying to transform your parenting, as well. Simply resolving on January 1st that, from that day forward, you are going to be a gentle parent and trying to change everything all at once is just setting yourself up for disappointment, frustration, and, more than likely, failure, followed by that age-old enemy of peace…mommy guilt.

Instead, try setting yourself up for success by taking a year of 'baby steps' to create real, lasting transformation in your parenting. Here are twelve steps you can start any time of the year, not just on January 1st, that offer practical, effective guidance to help you on your journey to gentle parenting. Keep in mind, though, that failure is a natural, normal part of change, so remember to give yourself grace when you fail. (Also, giving yourself grace is good practice for learning to extend that same grace to your children, which is a hallmark of gentle parenting!)

January (Step 1)

Slow down! ~ Gentle parenting is, at its core, based on a strong, healthy parent/child connection, so intentionally including time in your life to build and maintain that connection is vital. Start the year off by examining your daily and weekly schedule and looking for things to reduce or eliminate. Add up how much time your children spend in school, sleeping, in daycare, with babysitters, at sports practices, in music lessons, etc. and look at how much or little time is left over. Time for your family to connect, time to play, time to simply be, are just as important as those other activities, if not more so! Eliminate and reduce what you can, and look for ways to build connection into the things you can't eliminate. For instance, if your child has homework each night, why not sit down and work through the homework with them? As humans, we learn better through interaction, anyway, so you'll not only be connecting, you'll be enriching your child's education in the process! Another area that might benefit from a connection 'rehab' is that morning rush to get ready and out the door. Try getting everyone up a half hour earlier to ease the morning stresses that often lead to conflict and can result in a parent/child disconnect.

February (Step 2)

Listen! ~ Once you've slowed down enough to breathe, it's time to stretch yourself and grow as a parent. Like most changes in life, it won't come easy, but the rewards are well worth it. Fred Rogers said, "Listening is where love begins," meaning that when we listen, we really get to know someone, learn about what motivates them, and understand their thoughts, hopes, dreams, hurts, disappointments, etc. All behaviors communicate underlying needs, and what we learn about the inner life of our children by listening to them will help us to focus on the needs behind the behaviors instead of simply correcting the 'symptoms' (i.e. the behavior).

As a parent, it may seem instinctive to insist that our children listen to us so that our guidance and/or correction can be heard. In fact, the number one complaint I get from most parents is, "My children just don't listen!" to which I respond, "Do you?" The reality is that if a child doesn't feel they are being heard, then even if they stand silently 'listening' while we lecture or rant or even just talk, the child is simply rehearsing in their brain what they want to say rather than actually doing any effective listening. As the only adults in the parent/child relationship, it's up to the parent to be the first to listen, to *really* listen, because we are the ones with the maturity and self-control to be able to patiently wait to be heard.

March (Step 3)

Live what you want them to learn! ~ Ralph Waldo Emerson said, "What you do speaks so loud that I cannot hear what you say." Consciously, intentionally, and consistently living out how you want your children to turn out is the most powerful and effective character training there is. If you want your children to be kind, be kind. If you want them to be respectful, respect them. If you want them to learn self-control, model self-control. If you want them to be compassionate, treat them with compassion. If you want them to feel joy, enjoy them. If you want them to feel valuable, treasure them. The bottom line is, your children are always watching and learning, so make sure what they see in you is what you want to see in them!

April (Step 4)

Breathe! ~ We all get overwhelmed by the seemingly endless demands of life at times, so this month remind yourself to relax and consciously focus on enjoying your children. It's just a fact of human nature that when we enjoy something, we pay more attention to it, value it, and treat it better. Applying that fact to parenting, it makes sense to be intentional about taking time to laugh and hug and simply be with our children. Check out the 'bucket list' in Chapter Fifteen of *Two Thousand Kisses a Day: Gentle Parenting Through the Ages and Stages* full of ideas for simple, memorable fun to share with life's most precious treasures, your children!

May (Step 5)

Book it! ~ It's been said that our treasure lies where our time, attention, and love is invested. While having special family outings and activities is a wonderful way to enjoy our children, it is in the daily routines and busyness of life that the parent/child connection can often suffer the most. One of the best ways to stay connected with our children is to build time into each day to invest in them, and one of the best investments is in a love of reading. It's been said that the love of reading is born on the lap of a parent, in the soothing cadence of a mother's voice reading the same beloved story night after night, in the rhythmic sway of a rocking chair, and in the comfortable rustle of well-worn pages being turned one after another after another. A quiet bedtime routine that includes a nighttime story will not only help bedtime to be happier and smoother, but will also incorporate vital time for you to reconnect with your children at the end of every day.

June (Step 6)

Turn your no's into yes's! ~ In any home, like in any civilized society, boundaries are necessary for everyone's safety and comfort. With gentle parenting, setting limits focuses on connection and empathetic communication rather than control and punitive consequences. This month try setting limits using gentle parenting by turning your *no's* into *yes's*. Instead of *"No, you can't have ice cream until after dinner,"* try *"I know you love ice cream. I do, too! We're getting ready to eat right now, but what flavor would you like after dinner?"* This invites cooperation instead of triggering opposition, another hallmark of gentle parenting.

July (Step 7)

Play! ~ They say that the family that plays together, stays together, and there's great truth to that. Play is the language of childhood, and through play we get to know and connect with our children on their turf, in their native language, and on their terms. It's a powerful moment in a parent's life when they suddenly see their sweet little one as a separate, intelligent, worthy human being who can plan, make decisions, snap out orders, and lead other humans on a journey through an imaginary rainforest or on a trip through outer space. This month, try taking on the role of follower in your child's land of make-believe, and you'll discover a whole new world in which your child is strong, confident, and capable, and you'll come away with a deeper connection with and appreciation for the *person*, not just the child.

August (Step 8)

Eat well! ~ Along with all of the exercise you'll be getting playing with your child, take stock of the kinds of food you're providing to fuel their little engines and enrich their minds. Good nutrition may not be the first thought that pops into people's minds when they think of gentle parenting, but studies have shown that many behavior issues and sleep problems have their root in unhealthy eating habits, nutrient-poor diets, and food additives (dyes, preservatives, etc.). Children, especially littler ones, don't take change well as a general rule, and changes to the foods they eat are on top of the list of changes they'll resist. As a gentle parent, working with, instead of against, our children will help to make eating healthy a fun family project instead of a food fight. Try letting your children help you make weekly menus and shop for the fresh ingredients you'll be using, and let them help you cook, too. If they feel like they are a part of the change instead of a victim of it, they're far more likely to cooperate. If you have picky eaters, don't hesitate to serve them the same foods you normally do, just with a few added healthy ingredients slipped in to make them healthier. (For ideas on ways to make healthy changes more fun, check out Chapter Nine of *Two Thousand Kisses a Day: Gentle Parenting Through the Ages and Stages*)

September (Step 9)

Don't forget your funny bone! ~ Often the best parenting advice is simply, *"Chill out! Relax! Laugh a little, for goodness' sake!"* Sometimes as parents we get so caught up in 'fixing' our children that all we see are problems. We start focusing so much on preparing our children for their future that we forget to let them live in the present. One of the main problems with that is that children are, by their very nature, creatures of the 'now,' living fully immersed in each present moment. This month, pull out your dusty, old funny-bone, the one that used to keep you in stitches when you were a child, and laugh, on purpose, every day with your child. You'll be amazed at how a good belly laugh can turn even the worst day into something a little easier to handle and how much a giggle-fest can heal the little rifts that tend to occur in the parent/child connection throughout each day.

October (Step 10)

If you build it, they will come! ~ A shared project can offer a real chance to get to know your child on an entirely new level, so this month find something to build together. Choose something they are interested in, whether it's a model rocket or tree fort, and watch them blossom as they learn and build and grow. Your role is supportive--finding the materials, helping to read the instructions, offering suggestions or help when they struggle, etc. Simply being there through the process will enrich your connection with your child and offer you valuable insights into their interests and learning style, which will provide tools for you to use when helping them with their homework or if you are homeschooling them.

November (Step 11)

Gratitude is an attitude! ~ Teaching our children to be grateful involves far more than simply instructing them to say, *"Thank you."* We all want to be appreciated, and children are no different. Remember, modeling the things we want to see in our children is the single most powerful mode of instruction, so living a life of gratitude ourselves goes a long way toward raising our little ones to be happy, grateful humans. Openly appreciating our children, telling them what we like about them, and thanking them for the things they do is a sure-fire way of inspiring an attitude of gratitude in their little hearts. This month, be intentional in finding things to praise in your children. Don't be falsely enthusiastic or use *"Good job!"* as a brush-off to get them to leave you alone. Instead, honestly tell them what you like about them. Tell them *"Thank you"* when they remember to brush their teeth without being told or help their little sister with her block tower. Let them know you think their artwork is beautiful and don't hesitate to give them a pat on the back for a job well done when they straighten their room. Remember, it is the hungry child, not the satisfied child, who craves food, and, in the same way, it is *unmet* needs that lead to attention seeking behaviors and *unspoken* approval that can create 'praise junkies' as the unpraised child seeks to fill the very human need we all have for validation.

December (Step 12)

Celebrate! ~ Take time this month to give yourself a pat on the back for working toward your goal of becoming a gentle parent. Congratulate yourself for all that you've accomplished and take stock of your successes as well as your failures. Don't focus on your mistakes. Simply learn from them, forgive yourself, and move forward. Look back at where you were as a parent a year ago and compare that to where you are now. Don't worry if you haven't come as far as you'd like. Remember to give yourself grace. Life is for living and learning and growing, and another year is about to start with a chance to move forward into a new beginning. Everything you've invested in your children in the last year has been worthwhile, and everything you'll invest in the coming years will build on the foundation you've begun. So take this month to celebrate *you* and to enjoy the return on your investment!

~~~~~~~~

Do you see a theme throughout this gentle parenting '12-step program'? Getting to know and enjoy your children as individuals, intentionally focusing on building and maintaining a strong and healthy parent/child connection, and living what you want your children to learn are the bedrocks of gentle parenting. Walking through these steps, revisiting them when you find yourself struggling, and appreciating the incredible, miraculous gifts that each individual child brings into the world will keep you growing as a gentle parent day after day, month after month, year after year.

Live. Laugh. Love. Enjoy!

DISCUSSION QUESTIONS

1.   What does authority mean to you? How does that affect your daily life? How does your conception of authority affect your relationship with God? How does your conception of authority affect your relationship with your spouse, your supervisor at work, and/or your church leaders? How does your conception of authority affect your relationship with your children?

2.   What does submission mean to you? How does that affect your daily life? How does your understanding of submission affect your relationship with God? How does your understanding of submission affect your relationship with your spouse, your supervisor at work, and/or your church leaders? How does your understanding of submission affect your relationship with your children?

3.   What does sin mean to you? How does God respond to sin? How does your conception of sin affect your daily life? How does your conception of sin affect your relationship with God? How does your conception of sin affect your parenting?

4.   What does sin nature mean to you? How does your understanding of sin nature affect your relationship with God? How does your understanding of sin nature affect your parenting?

5.   What does obedience mean to you? How does your conception of obedience affect your relationship with God? How does your conception of obedience affect your relationship with your children?

6.   What does fear mean to you? How does your definition of fear affect your conception of God? How does that affect your relationship with God? How does that translate to your relationship with your children?

7. What does free will mean to you? How does that function in your daily life? How does your free will affect your relationship with God? How does free will affect your relationship with your children?

8. What does faith mean to you? How does that affect your daily life? How does your conception of faith affect your relationship with God?

9. What does love mean to you? How does your understanding of love affect your relationship with God? How does your understanding of love affect your relationship with your children?

10. What does grace mean to you? How does grace function in your daily life? How does your understanding of grace affect your relationship with God? How does your understanding of grace affect your relationship with your children? How can you model grace for your children?

11. What does the parenthood of God mean to you? How does your conception of God as a Father affect your relationship with him? How does your conception of God as a Father affect your relationship with your children?

12. What are your short-term goals for your children? What are your long-term goals for your children? How are your parenting choices accomplishing your goals?

POINTS TO PONDER

- We have the Father…not a father, but THE Father…to look to for guidance about how to parent our children.

- Everything, absolutely everything, in raising children is dependent upon a secure parent/child relationship, and the foundation is trust.

- If perfection were possible, the Cross wouldn't have been necessary.

- My failures remind me to turn to my perfect Parent, God, and trust him with my children. And my failures offer me the opportunity to be transparent with my children, to ask for forgiveness, to show them it's okay to be human and to make mistakes.

- We just can't wrap our human brains around something as awesomely simple as unconditional love. We think it *must* be more complicated, and we end up complicating it by trying to pay for something that is free.

- Your children are a reward, a blessing, a gift straight from the heart of your Father to you, his precious child. He wants you to feel what he feels, to experience him in a unique way through parenting your children in the way that he parents you. He wants you to delight in your children so you'll understand how he delights in you. He wants you to feel the depth of concern He feels when you stray into danger, the heights of joy He feels when you run trustingly into His arms, the pangs of compassion he feels when you are hurting or scared. Take the time to enjoy your children, and you will find yourself closer to the heart of your Father than you can possibly imagine.

- Parenthood is, very simply, a beautiful sacrifice that mothers and fathers willingly and lovingly live for their children, day after day, night after night, as a reflection of the sacrifice Jesus made for his children on the Cross. Parenthood is a lovely, lively retelling of the Cross played out in the arms of mamas and daddies, again and again and again.

- Life is messy. No one has all the answers, at least not earth-side. But we can all trust that this sometimes bewildering, sometimes joyful, sometimes flat-out painful chaos called life has meaning and purpose and beauty beyond the scope of human sight. And as we carefully and gently weave the strands of our children's days into a beautiful childhood, we can trust that our Father is thoughtfully and tenderly doing the same for us.

- Sin nature, in and of itself, is not sin. It is, instead, the *capability* to sin. It is only in our choices when we are old enough to be conscious of sin, in how we use God's gift of free will, that sin enters the picture. And it is on the cross, not in an establishment of authority, not in a demand for obedience, not in a display of power, but in the love of a gentle Savior, that sin exits the picture.

- We are our children's first experience of God. How we treat them, how we respond to them, what we model for them, those are all images of parenthood that are imprinted on our children's hearts from the moment of birth, and they will carry those images with them for life. God's unconditional love, his gentleness, his compassion, his acceptance, his sacrifice…those are the images our children need to see reflected in our parenting, to have tenderly woven into the fabric of their childhood, to carry forever as whispered memories etched on their hearts, echoing the heart of God.

- Mary didn't practice attachment parenting as she was growing a tiny Savior. She simply parented Jesus in the naturally instinctive way that mothers have mothered their little ones since time began.

- Breastfeeding is a biological norm created by God to meet a baby's needs in the healthiest and most convenient way.

- Humans don't learn to soothe themselves by being left to soothe themselves. We were designed by a relational God to be relational beings and, therefore, to learn and grow and have our needs met through our relationships, both with him, our heavenly Father, and with our earthly parents.

- In God's perfect design, peace and contentment are shared from parent to child, not through ignoring needs, but through meeting needs. Our little ones don't need to be trained to soothe themselves to sleep; they need to be parented to sleep by our soothing presence, comfort, and support.

- The Three C's of gentle parenting are Connection, Communication, and Cooperation, with connection being the starting point. Building that connection through babywearing in the first weeks and months and years, keeping our little ones close enough for kisses and smiles and cuddles throughout the day, is not only convenient, it's also a beautiful picture of how God carries us close to his heart and a lovely way of conveying the image of an always close, always available, always loving heavenly Father.

- The meaning of what is now translated *obey* in the original text of the Bible is more accurately read 'listen to, thoughtfully consider, and respond to.'

- The word used in English translations of the Bible, *punish*, conveys an external infliction of negative consequences, while the original words, *avon* (Hebrew) and *kolasis/kolazo* (Greek) convey internal, self-imposed consequences (i.e. carrying the weight of guilt/shame) and natural consequences (i.e. being estranged).

- Just as God is *"our refuge and our strength"* and *"an ever-present help"* that is what we need to be for our children, to reflect the heart of our Father to our own little ones.

- Either grace is sufficient for all or it is sufficient for none. There is no in-between. You are your children's first taste of God, their first understanding of love, their first vision of grace. How you treat them in that capacity will inevitably affect their relationship with Christ. Choose love, because he is Love in the flesh. Choose gentleness, because he is the

Gentle Shepherd. Choose grace, because he died so that you could.

- God stepped right down in the flesh for skin-to-skin time with his children. In Jesus, he lived and slept and walked with his children day and night, always available, meeting every need whether it was food, healing, guidance, or comfort.

- Do you really believe that Jesus' New Covenant is for everyone *except* children? That grace, mercy, unconditional love, and forgiveness are for adults only? The disciples made that mistake, and Jesus said to them, *"Let the little children come to me, and do not hinder them, for the kingdom of God belongs to such as these." (Luke 18:16)*

- Let's choose gentleness in our parenting so that we let our *"gentleness be evident to all"* including (especially!) our littlest, most defenseless, and truly precious gifts from God—our children.

- Conferring negative and critical attitudes toward children has incalculable potential to damage the parent/child relationship. And yet it is that very relationship that should reflect our trust relationship with God, including reflecting his delight in his children. God's love is unconditional, and ours should be, as well.

- Children are people. Period. And they are people that *matter*. Their likes and dislikes *matter*. Their interests *matter*. Their opinions *matter*. When they are externally controlled, ordered to obey instantly and cheerfully to every command that they are given, their personhood is disregarded and their in-built human instinct, that God-given free will that makes us the individuals that we were created to be, is to resist those external controls.

- Telling a child, or showing them through our disregard, that something they care about isn't important doesn't convince them that it doesn't matter. It just convinces them that it doesn't matter to *us*, and they often begin to feel that they don't matter to us, either.

- Our will is a *gift*, an opportunity to *choose* right from wrong, and the vehicle through which God calls us to choose his Son. Without this amazing and wonderful gift, without the freedom to use our free will, Jesus' suffering and death on the Cross would be pointless.

- Sin is a moot point in light of the grace we've been given. Grace is the point. The *whole* point. Everything leading up to the Cross pointed to the Cross, everything was settled on the Cross, and on the Cross in the outstretched arms of Jesus grace was born. Sin only matters in the sense that when we voluntarily choose to stay within the boundaries God has given us, we are closer to him, more in-tune with him, and more aligned with his will.

- Most behavior challenges can be avoided if we simply start out by listening. We are the only adults in the relationship, and it is up to us to exercise patience, to slow down and get down and give our little ones our time and attention and really hear them. It can be challenging at times, for sure, to understand what our children are trying to say, really say, when their words and actions can seem so unreasonable to the adult mind. But if we listen with our hearts, our eyes, our ears, all of our senses, we will see and hear and understand. Frustrations will fade. Conflicts will cease. Hearts will heal. And the connection that leads to cooperation will be established, with communication as the vehicle.

- We're human. We're imperfect. With Jesus as the measuring stick, we will always come up short. Luckily for us, we have a Father who loves us just as we are instead of measuring us to see what we aren't.

- Aren't we emptying the Cross of its power and its message when we insist that our children must bear the consequences of their mistakes? We've been freed from the consequences of *our* mistakes. Don't we want our children to have the same experience, the same *freely offered* gift?

- The world will hurt, disappoint, and disillusion our children through the years, no doubt, but the brief season of childhood is a time to strengthen our children, not weaken them, and true strength is forged in gentleness, guided by wisdom, and steeped in peace.

- Our children are watching how we live far more than they are hearing what we say. They are learning how to live by our choices, not by our words

- God doesn't hate the sin but love the sinner. He hates the sin because he loves his child.

- Forgiveness empties the past of its power to empty the present of its peace.

- Forgiving someone doesn't mean telling them that hurting us was okay. It means telling ourselves that it's okay to stop hurting. It doesn't mean we have to trust them again. It means we can learn to trust ourselves again because we deserve it. It doesn't mean we have to give them a free pass back into our lives. It means we are free to take our lives back again.

- Guilt is destructive, not constructive. Holding onto our guilt over past mistakes doesn't make up for those mistakes and it doesn't help us to avoid repeating those mistakes. In fact, just the opposite. Holding onto guilt keeps us in a constant state of pain which can then fester and either explode into angry outbursts or implode into self-destructive behaviors such as addictions, depression, self-harm, eating disorders, inability to feel love, etc.

- We are imperfect humans growing imperfect humans in an imperfect world, and that's perfectly okay.

- When children are treated with kindness, respect, and compassion, they are far more likely carry the seeds of kindness, respect, and compassion into the world with them and plant them in the hearts and lives of others they meet on their journey through life.

- Growing kind children starts at home by being kind *to* our children. Gentleness, faithfulness, and self-control have their roots at home, in *our own* behavior. Joy and peace are flowing springs that we can share with our children to grow them into healthy adults who will change the world instead of being changed by the world. The adults we send out into the world will reflect the love, joy, peace, patience, kindness, goodness, faithfulness, gentleness, and self-control they experience from us at home.

- Responding to our children's challenging behaviors with challenging behaviors of our own is not only simply throwing fuel on a fire, it's also the polar opposite of the call to be peacemakers, to be imitators of Christ who, even from the Cross, whispered words of peace, comfort, and forgiveness.

- We are, every one of us, inclined toward the full range of human behaviors and emotions, both positive and negative. We were created that way, and everything God creates is good. Yes, you read that right. We are *good*. But we can *do* bad. That is human nature. That is free will. And that is beautiful, messy, wonder-filled, chaotic, lovely, noisy, joyful, heartbreaking life here on earth.

- God, Love Himself, has made us acceptable *because* he loves us, not so that he *can* love us.

- Remember, parents, *we* are our children's first taste of God, and his wondrous, miraculous delight in his children's delight is an integral part of who he is and how he relates to us. Let's be reflectors of his goodness and love, conveyors of his acceptance and forgiveness, conduits for his grace and mercy.

- Focusing on sin puts the emphasis on the consequences of sin instead of on the Cross. It makes avoiding sin the point instead of seeking the Cross the point. But humans don't have a great track record of avoiding sin. In fact, sin is inevitable as long as we are here in our present state. If that weren't true, then perfection would be possible and the Cross would be pointless.

- Grace-focused parenting creates a safe environment to grow and learn and explore, to make mistakes and learn from those mistakes. And, with every forgiven mistake, with every outpouring of grace, the Cross grows ever nearer and dearer to their hearts.

- It's never too late to begin building the trust relationship that underpins grace-based parenting, just as it's never too late for us to receive grace from and walk in accord with our Father.

- Focusing on sin is pointless because sin is a moot point. Grace is and always will be the point...the *only* point. And, interestingly enough, when avoiding sin is not the focus, its hold loosens on all of us.

- So often when we read God's Word we hear what we've heard from the pulpit instead of hearing the voice of a Father who loves unconditionally, sacrificially, and eternally. And so often what we've heard from the pulpit is accusation, damnation, and condemnation. It's no wonder we have problems trusting in God's unconditional love if all we hear are commands, demands, and reprimands echoed in those misguided voices.

- Humans aren't perfect and, no matter how wise, how conscientious, how educated they are, the simple fact is that the human mind cannot fully grasp the mind and heart of God and, therefore, their interpretations of the Bible must always be regarded with careful examination instead of absolute faith.

- Listen for the still, small voice of love, wisdom, and guidance from God, the *only* source of truth. The viewpoints, analysis, and interpretations of scripture that you've read here in *Jesus, the Gentle Parent*, like all others, must be examined, discussed, and prayed over instead of taken on faith. Keep your faith for God alone. When you read the words in this book, don't accept them. Question them. Challenge them. Test them. Pray about them. Ask God to give you eyes to see and ears to hear so that you can make your own decisions based on God's wise and wonderful counsel.

SCRIPTURES REFERENCED

"Let your gentleness be evident to all." Philippians 4:5 NIV

"But the greatest of these is love" 1 Corinthians 13:13 NIV

"…a great and powerful wind tore the mountains apart and shattered the rocks before the Lord, but the Lord was not in the wind. After the wind there was an earthquake, but the Lord was not in the earthquake. After the earthquake came a fire, but the Lord was not in the fire. And after the fire came a gentle whisper…" 1 Kings 19:11 NIV

"Whoever receives one of these little children in My name receives Me; and whoever receives Me, receives not Me but Him who sent Me." Mark 9:37 ESV

"For I know the plans I have for you," declares the Lord, "plans to prosper you and not to harm you, plans to give you hope and a future." Jeremiah 29:11 NIV

"Now we see through a glass darkly; then we shall see clearly, face to face. Now I know in part, then I shall know fully, even as I am fully known." 1 Corinthians 13:12 KJV

"Before I created you in the womb I knew you; before you were born I set you apart"
Jeremiah 1:5 CEB

"God saw all that he had made, and it was very good" Genesis 1:31 NIV

"It is finished." John 19:30 NIV

"Follow God's example, therefore, as dearly loved children and walk in the way of love, just as Christ loved us and gave himself up for us as a fragrant offering and sacrifice to God." Ephesians 5:1-2 NIV

"But we proved to be gentle among you, as a nursing mother tenderly cares for her own children." 1 Thessalonians 2:7 NASB

"Blessed is the mother who gave you birth and nursed you." Luke 11:27 NIV

"For you will nurse and be satisfied at her comforting breasts." Isaiah 66:11 NIV

"For I was hungry and you gave me something to eat, I was thirsty and you gave me something to drink, I was a stranger and you invited me in, I needed clothes and you clothed me, I was sick and you looked after me..." Matthew 25:35-40 NIV

"You shall call, and the Lord will answer; You shall cry, and he will say, 'Here I am.'"
Isaiah 58:9 ESV

"When they cry out to me, I will hear, for I am compassionate," Exodus 22:27 NIV

"I am he who comforts you," Isaiah 51:12 ESV

"Praise be to the Father of compassion and the God of all comfort, who comforts us in all our troubles, so that we can comfort those in any trouble with the comfort we ourselves receive from God." 2 Corinthians 1:3-4 NIV

"Do not fear, for I am with you; do not be afraid, for I am your God. I will strengthen you; I will help you; I will hold on to you with my righteous right hand."
Isaiah 41:10 HCSB

"He tends his flock like a shepherd He gathers the lambs in his arms and carries them close to his heart." Isaiah 40:11 NIV

"Look also at ships: although they are so large and are driven by fierce winds, they are turned by a very small rudder wherever the pilot desires." James 3:4 ESV

"You will know them by their fruit." Matthew 7:16 ESV

He replied, "Blessed rather are those who hear the Word of God and obey (listen to, thoughtfully consider, and respond to) it." Luke 11:28 NIV

Jesus replied, "Anyone who loves me will obey (listen to, thoughtfully consider, and respond to) my teaching. My Father will love them, and we will come to them and make our home with them. John 14:23 NIV

"Children, obey (listen to, thoughtfully consider, and respond to) your parents in the Lord, for this is right." Ephesians 6:1 NIV

"There is no fear in love. But perfect love drives out fear, because fear has to do with punishment (bearing one's own iniquity, carrying guilt, feeling shame, being estranged)." 1 John 4:18 NIV

"For I am the Lord your God who takes hold of your right hand and says to you, Do not fear; I will help you." Isaiah 41:13 NIV

"Jesus entered the temple courts and drove out all who were buying and selling there. He overturned the tables of the money changers and the benches of those selling doves. "It is written," he said to them, "'My house will be called a house of prayer but you are making it a den of robbers.'" Matthew 21:12-13 NIV

"In your anger do not sin: Do not let the sun go down while you are still angry, and do not give the devil a foothold." Ephesians 4:26-27 NIV

"God is our refuge and strength, an ever-present help in times of trouble." Psalm 46:1 GWT

"Let the little children come to me, and do not hinder them, for the kingdom of God belongs to such as these." Luke 18:16 NIV

"Whatever you have learned or received or heard from me, or seen in me—put it into practice." Philippians 4:9 NIV

"Therefore be imitators of God as dear children. And walk in love, as Christ also has loved us and given Himself for us, an offering and a sacrifice to God." Ephesians 5:1-2 NKJV

"Train up (introduce a child to/set a child on the path) in the way he should go, and when he is old he will not depart from it." Proverbs 22:6 ESV

"The Lord is good to all; he has compassion on all he has made." Psalm 145:9 NIV

"Your rod and your staff, they comfort me…" Psalm 23:4 NIV

"He who spares his rod (wisdom, leadership, protection) hates (does not love, does not choose/show a preference for) his son, but he who loves him disciplines (offers verbal instruction and teaching to) him promptly." Proverbs 13:24 NKJV

"Foolishness (naivety, silliness, inexperience) is bound up in the heart of a child (young man); the rod of correction (wisdom, leadership, protection) will drive it far from him." Proverbs 22:15 KJV

"The rod (wisdom, leadership, protection) and rebuke (reasoning with, convincing, proving, persuading) give wisdom, but a child (young man) left to himself brings shame to his mother." Proverbs 29:15 ISV

"Apply your heart to instruction and your ears to words of knowledge.
Do not withhold discipline (verbal instruction and teaching, reasoning together) from a child (young man);
if you punish (guide, trigger his conscience, favorably impress, entice/entrance) them with the rod (wisdom, leadership, protection), they will not die (follow a path of destruction).
Punish (guide, trigger his conscience, favorably impress, entice/entrance) them with the rod (wisdom, leadership, protection) and save them from death (following a path of destruction).
My son, if your heart is wise, then my heart will be glad indeed;
my inmost being will rejoice when your lips speak what is right.
Do not let your heart envy sinners, but always be zealous for the fear of the Lord.
There is surely a future hope for you, and your hope will not be cut off.
Listen, my son, and be wise, and set your heart on the right path:
Do not join those who drink too much wine or gorge themselves on meat, for drunkards and gluttons become poor, and drowsiness clothes them in rags.
Listen to your father, who gave you life, and do not despise your mother when she is old.
Buy the truth and do not sell it—wisdom, instruction and insight as well.
The father of a righteous child young man has great joy; a man who fathers a wise son rejoices in him.
May your father and mother rejoice; may she who gave you birth be joyful!
My son, give me your heart and let your eyes delight in my ways." Proverbs 23:12-26 NIV

"Ministers of a new covenant—not of the letter but of the Spirit; for the letter kills, but the Spirit gives life." 2 Corinthians 3:6 NIV

"Not on tablets of stone but on tablets of human hearts." 2 Corinthians 3:3 NIV

"For whoever keeps the whole law and yet stumbles at just one point is guilty of breaking all of it." James 2:10 NIV

"The fruit of the Spirit is love, joy, peace, patience, kindness, goodness, faithfulness, gentleness, and self-control" Galatians 5:22-23 NIV

"This is how God showed his great love for us, that Christ died for us while we were still sinners" Romans 5:8 ESV

"At that time Jesus, full of joy through the Holy Spirit, said, 'I praise you, Father, Lord of heaven and earth, because you have hidden these things from the wise and learned, and revealed them to little children.'" Luke 10:21 NIV

"Do not be anxious about anything, but in every situation, by prayer and petition, with thanksgiving, present your requests to God. And the peace of God, which passes understanding, will guard your hearts and your minds in Christ Jesus." Philippians 4:6-7 NIV

"Be completely humble and gentle; be patient, bearing with one another in love." Ephesians 4:2 NIV

"Love is patient, love is kind. It does not envy, it does not boast, it is not proud. It does not dishonor others, it is not self-seeking, it is not easily angered, it keeps no record of wrongs." 1 Corinthians 13:4-5 NIV

"Still other seed fell on good soil. It came up, grew and produced a crop, some multiplying thirty, some sixty, some a hundred times." Mark 4:8 NIV

"I will exalt you; I will praise your name, for you have done wonderful things, plans formed of old, faithful and sure." Isaiah 25:1 ESV

"Like a city whose walls are broken through is a person who lacks self-control." Proverbs 25:28 NIV

"See that you do not look down on one of these little ones. For I tell you that their angels in heaven always see the face of my Father in heaven." Matthew 18: 10 HCSB

"Are not five sparrows sold for two pennies? And not one of them is forgotten before God. Why, even the hairs of your head are all numbered. Fear not; you are of more value than many sparrows." Luke 12:6-7 NASB

"I cried out to the Lord with my voice, and he heard me from his Holy mountain" Psalm 3:4 NKJV

"Let us then approach God's throne of grace with confidence, so that we may receive mercy and find grace to help us in our time of need." Hebrews 4:16 NIV

"I stand at the door and knock. If anyone hears my voice and opens the door, I will come in and eat with that person, and they with me." Revelations 3:20 NIV

"I have set before you life and death, blessing and curse; therefore choose life, that you and your descendants may live." Deuteronomy 30:19 NETB

"Draw near to God and He will draw near to you." James 4:8 ESV

"The Lord's loving-kindnesses indeed never cease, for his compassions never fail." Lamentations 3:22 NASB

"Because he bends down to listen, I will pray as long as I have breath." Psalm 116:2 NLT

"Wisdom from above is first pure, then peaceable, gentle, open to reason, full of mercy and good fruits, impartial and sincere." James 3:17 ESV

"Morning, noon, and night I complain and groan, and he listens to my voice." Psalm 55:17 GWT

"I do not set aside the grace of God, for if righteousness could be gained through the law, Christ died for nothing!" Galatians 2:21 NIV

"Peace I leave with you; my peace I give you. I do not give to you as the world gives. Do not let your hearts be troubled and do not be afraid." John 14:27 NIV

"Truly I tell you, unless you change and become like little children, you will never enter the kingdom of heaven." Matthew 18:3 NIV

"While we were yet sinners, Christ died for us." Romans 5:8 NASV

"The fear of the Lord is the beginning of wisdom," Proverbs 9:10 NIV

"In everything, do to others what you would have them do to you, for this sums up the Law and the Prophets." Matthew 7:12 NIV

"Come now, let us reason together" Isaiah 1:18 ESV

"Therefore, as God's chosen people, holy and dearly loved, clothe yourselves with compassion, kindness, humility, gentleness and patience." Colossians 3:12 NIV

"Therefore if you have any encouragement from being united with Christ, if any comfort from his love, if any common sharing in the Spirit, if any tenderness and compassion, then make my joy complete by being like-minded, having the same love, being one in spirit and of one mind." Philippians 2:1-2 NIV

"But no discipline (instruction) in its time seems to be joyful, but it is sorrowful (difficult, hard work); but in the end it yields the fruit of peace and of righteousness" Hebrews 12:11 NASB

"But if anyone obeys (understands, reflects upon, is persuaded by) his word, love for God is truly made complete in them. This is how we know we are in him." 1 John 2:5 NIV

"Submit to (agree with, compromise with, be at peace with) one another out of reverence for Christ." Ephesians 5:21 NIV

"There is no longer Jew or Gentile, slave or free, male and female. For you are all one in Christ Jesus." Galatians 3:28 NIV

"Even the Son of Man came not to be served but to serve." Mark 10:45 NIV

"Come to me, all you who are weary and burdened, and I will give you rest. Take my yoke upon you and learn from me, for I am gentle and humble in heart, and you will find rest for your souls. For my yoke is easy and my burden is light." Matthew 11:28-30 NIV

"A new commandment I give to you, that you love one another, even as I have loved you, that you also love one another." John 13:34 NASB

"Put on then, as God's chosen ones, holy and beloved, compassionate hearts, kindness, humility, meekness, and patience, bearing with one another and, if one has a complaint against another, forgiving each other; as the Lord has forgiven you, so you also must forgive. And above all these put on love, which binds everything together in perfect harmony." Colossians 3:12-14 ESV

"Therefore, there is now no condemnation for those who are in Christ Jesus." Romans 8:1 NIV

"I praise you because I am fearfully and wonderfully made; your works are wonderful, I know that full well." Psalm 139:14 NIV

"There are different kinds of spiritual gifts, but the same Spirit is the source of them all." 1 Corinthians 12:4 NLT

"Be kind to one another, tenderhearted, forgiving one another, as God in Christ forgave you." Ephesians 4:32 ESV

"'Love the Lord your God with all your heart and with all your soul and with all your strength and with all your mind'; and, 'Love your neighbor as yourself...' Which of these three do you think was a neighbor to the man?'... The expert in the law replied, 'The one who had mercy on him.' Jesus told him, 'Go and do likewise.'" Luke 10:27-28 & 37 NIV

"Blessed are the peacemakers: for they shall be called the children of God." Matthew 5:9 KJV

""You heard my cry for mercy when I called to you for help" Psalm 31:22 NIV

"Love is patient, love is kind. It does not envy, it does not boast, it is not proud. It does not dishonor others, it is not self-seeking, it is not easily angered, it keeps no record of wrongs. Love does not delight in evil but rejoices with the truth. It always protects, always trusts, always hopes, always perseveres." 1 Corinthians 13:4-8 NIV

"See what kind of love the Father has given to us, that we should be called children of God; and so we are." 1 John 3:1 ESV

"Can a mother forget the baby at her breast and have no compassion on the child she has borne? Though she may forget, I will not forget you! See, I have engraved you on the palms of my hands" Isaiah 49:15-16 NIV

"There is no fear in love. But perfect love drives out fear, because fear has to do with punishment. The one who fears is not made perfect in love." 1 John 4:18 NIV

"I came that they may have life, and have it abundantly." John 10:10 ESV

"Every good thing given and every perfect gift is from above, coming down from the Father of lights, with whom there is no variation or shifting shadow." James 1:17 NASB

"Taste and see that the Lord is good" Psalm 34:8 NIV

"If anyone hears my words but does not keep them, I do not judge that person. For I did not come to judge the world, but to save the world." John 12:47 NIV

"For it is by grace you have been saved, through faith--and this is not from yourselves, it is the gift of God" Ephesians 2:8 NIV

"Be still, and know that I am God." Psalm 46:10 NIV

"Be dressed in readiness, and keep your lamps lit." Luke 12:35 NASB

"The Lord's bond-servant must not be quarrelsome, but be kind to all, able to teach, patient when wronged."
2 Timothy 2:24 NASB

"But blessed are your eyes, because they see; and your ears, because they hear. For truly I say to you that many prophets and righteous men desired to see what you see, and did not see it, and to hear what you hear, and did not hear it." Matthew 13:16-17 NIV

"If I speak in the tongues of men and of angels, but have not love, I am a noisy gong or a clanging cymbal. And if I have prophetic powers, and understand all mysteries and all knowledge, and if I have all faith, so as to remove mountains, but have not love, I am nothing. If I give away all I have, and if I deliver up my body to be burned, but have not love, I Gain nothing. Love is patient and kind; love does not envy or boast; it is not arrogant or rude. It does not insist on its own way; it is not irritable or resentful; it does not rejoice at wrongdoing, but rejoices with the truth. Love bears all things, believes all things, hopes all things, endures all things. Love never ends." 1 Corinthians 13:1-8 ESV

"Now I know in part; then I shall know fully, even as I have been fully known. So now faith, hope, and love abide, these three; but the greatest of these is love." 1 Corinthians 13:12-13 ESV

"We speak the wisdom of God in a mystery, even the hidden wisdom which God ordained before the world to our glory" 1 Corinthians 2:7 AKJV

"For God so loved the world, that he gave his only Son, that whoever believes in him should not perish but have eternal life." John 3:16 NIV

HEBREW/GREEK LEXICON

Child:
(English) - an unborn or recently born person; an infant; a young person especially between infancy and youth; childlike or childish person; a person not yet of age; a minor
(Hebrew) *yeled* or *yaldah* - newborn boy or girl
yonek or *yanak* - nursling baby
olel – nursling baby who also eats food (translated 'young child' in Lamentations 4:4 KJV)
gamal - weaned child (around 3-4 years old)
taph - young child, one who still clings to their mother
elem or *almah* - firm and strong, older child
na'ar (masc.) or *na'arah* (fem.) - independent child, young adult child (includes older adolescents and young adults)
(Greek) *paidion* – little child
teknon – child, dependent, descendent

Command:
(English) - direct authoritatively; order; exercise a dominating influence over; have command of; have at one's immediate disposal; demand or receive as one's due
(Hebrew) *tsawah* – directions; guides; [having to do specifically with physical directions for a journey, i.e. finding the right path or way]; *mitzvah* – life lesson; precept; directions for a journey
(Greek) *entole* – guiding principle; life lesson; precept

Death/Destruction:
(English) – a permanent cessation of all vital functions; the end of life; the cause or occasion of loss of life; a cause of ruin
(Hebrew) *muwth* – die; death; bring death; destruction; follow a path of destruction

Discipline:
(English) – [originally] to teach, guide, instruct; [modern definition - train to obey rules or a code of behavior, using punishment to correct disobedience]
(Hebrew) *muwcar* - verbal instruction and teaching; [In Hebrew culture *muwcar* was vernacular for 'let us reason with one another' implying a mutual discussion for learning purposes]
(Greek) *paideuo* – nurture, grow, nourish, encourage

Disobey/Disobedience:
(English) - Failure or refusal to obey rules or someone in authority
(Hebrew) *parakouo* – to close one's ears to; to ignore
(Greek) *peitharcheo* – to remain unpersuaded; to be unmoved by; to be unresponsive to

Fear:
(English) – an unpleasant emotion caused by the belief that someone or something is dangerous, likely to cause pain, or a threat; feeling afraid; showing fear or anxiety; causing or likely to cause people to be afraid; horrifying
(Hebrew) *yirah* - to see or be seen with intense clarity and intentionality; have a heightened awareness of; wonder; amazement; mystery; astonishment; overflowing emotion

Foolishness:
(English) – lacking in sense, judgment, or discretion; absurd, ridiculous
(Hebrew) *ivveleth* - foolishness, inexperience, naivety, silliness.

Hate:
(English) – intense hostility and aversion usually deriving from fear, anger, or sense of injury; extreme dislike or antipathy; loathing
(Hebrew) *sane* - does not love; does not choose/show a preference for

Obey/Obedience:
(English) - comply with a command, direction, or request of an authority figure or a law; submit to the authority of
(Hebrew) *hupakouo/hupakoe* – to hear from above; to listen for; to lend an ear to; and *shama/lishmoa* – to understand, to internalize, to ponder, to reflect upon
(Greek) *peitho* – to be persuaded; to be moved; to respond

Praise:
(English) – to express a favorable judgment of; commend; to glorify especially by the attribution of perfections

(Hebrew) *halal* - to look toward another as a shining light; [as in *halelu-Yah* which means to "Look to Yah (the Lord) as the light that will guide you on your journey]

Proverb:

(English) - a short pithy saying in general use, stating a general truth or piece of advice

(Hebrew) *mashal* - a parable, prophetic and figurative discourse, symbolic poem, pithy maxim (i.e. a collection of wise metaphors and adages)

Punish:

(English) - to inflict a penalty upon; to exact retribution; to make suffer

(Hebrew) *avon* – to carry guilt; to bear one's own iniquity; *nakah* – beat [as in "The sun beat down on his head," implying a constant presence; or 'hit' as when beating back an enemy or punishing a slave or criminal; or 'smite or smitten' which can mean 'hit or 'trigger the conscience' or 'be favorably impressed, enticed, or entranced' as in, "He was smitten with the idea of a new bicycle"]

(Greek) *kolasis/kolazo* – removed; separated

Rebuke:

(English) – express sharp disapproval or criticism of (someone) because of their behavior or actions

(Hebrew) *towkechah* - reason with, convince, prove, persuade

Rod:

(English) – a straight, thin stick or bar; a stick used to hit or whip someone as a form of punishment

(Hebrew) shebet – shepherd's crook; [Denotes wisdom, leadership, protection; the shebet in Hebrew culture was a means not only of guiding and protecting sheep, but also a symbol of leadership. The markings on the head of the shebet often identified the head of a family or tribe, letting everyone know who to go to for guidance and protection.]

Sin:

(English) – an immoral act considered to be a transgression against divine law

(Hebrew) *chata'ah* - missing the mark; *pasha* - going beyond the limits; [i.e. miss God's mark, go beyond God's limits, not be within God's will]
(Greek) *hamartia* - not a part of; has no share in; [i.e. to depart from God, to operate outside of his nature]

Submit:
(English) – accepting or yielding to a superior force or to the will or authority of another
(Hebrew) *shema/lishmoa* - to listen, hear, attend, understand, internalize, respond
(Greek) *hupotasso* - to choose to agree with, to walk in accord; to work together; to compromise; to be at peace; to become one

Train:
(English) - teach a particular skill or type of behavior through practice and instruction over a period of time
(Hebrew) *chanak/chanokh* - dedicate, commit to special use, focus on a specific purpose; or initiate, introduce to, create an appetite or taste for, set on the path
(Greek) *paideuo* – nurture, grow, nourish, encourage

References:

1. Old Testament Hebrew Lexicon - New American Standard. (n.d.). *Theological Word Book of the Old Testament.* Retrieved , from **http://www.biblestudytools.com/lexicons/hebrew/nas/**
2. Benner, J. A. (2005). *The Ancient Hebrew Lexicon of the Bible: Hebrew Letters, Words and Roots Defined Within Their Ancient Cultural Context.* College Station, TX: Virtualbookworm.com Publishing.
3. Benner, J. A. (2004). *The Ancient Hebrew Language and Alphabet: Understanding the Ancient Hebrew Language of the Bible Based on Ancient Hebrew Culture and Thought.* College Station, TX: Virtualbookworm. com Publishing.
4. Tripp, T. (1995). *Shepherding a Child's Heart.* Wapwallopen, PA: Shepherd Press.
5. Dobson, J. C., & Dobson, J. C. (2004). *The New Strong-Willed Child: Birth Through Adolescence.* Wheaton, Ill.: Tyndale House Publishers.
6. Williams, R. E. (2011, April 25). *The Correction and Salvation of Children.* Retrieved April 15, 2014, from http://undermuchgrace.blogspot.com/2011/04/ron-williams-on-beating-infants.html
7. Boyle, A. (2013, June 13). *This is your brain on fatherhood: Dads experience hormonal changes too, research shows* - NBC News. NBC News. Retrieved April 15, 2014, from **http://www.nbcnews.com/science/science-news/your-brain-fatherhood-dads-experience-hormonal-changes-too-research-shows-f6C10333109**
8. Sánchez, Cristina L.; Cubero, Javier; Sánchez, Javier; Chanclón, Belén; Rivero, Montserrat; Rodríguez, Ana B.; Barriga, Carmen. "The possible role of human milk nucleotides as sleep inducers". Nutritional Neuroscience Vol. 12(1):2-8. 2009.
9. Melissa Bartick, MD, MSca, Arnold Reinhold, MBA, . "The Burden of Suboptimal Breastfeeding in the United States: A Pediatric Cost Analysis." Journal of the American Academy of Pediatrics . (2010): n. page. Web. 6 Feb. 2013. **http://pediatrics.aappublications.org/content/early/2010/04/05/peds.2009-1616.abstract**
10. Pullella, P. (2014, January 12). Breastfeed babies if you want, pope tells mothers in Sistine Chapel. *Reuters.* Retrieved April 15, 2014, from **http://www.reuters.com/article/2014/01/12/us-pope-baptism-idUSBREA0B05Z20140112**
11. Daly, Steven and Peter Hartmann. "Infant Demand and Milk Supply. Part 1: Infant Demand and Milk Production in Lactating Women." *Journal of Human Lactation I* l(l) 1995; p. 21-26.

12. Schore, A.N. (2000). Attachment and the regulation of the right brain. Attachment & Human Development, 2, 23-47.

13. M.S., C. W. (2014, March 11). Falling in Love With Your Baby. *Health Day*. Retrieved April 15, 2014, from **http://consumer.healthday.com/encyclopedia/parenting-31/parenting-health-news-525/falling-in-love-with-your-baby-643058.html**

14. Christensson K, Cabrera T, Christensson E, Uvnas-Moberg K, & Winberg J. Separation distress call in the human neonate in the absence of maternal body contact. Acta Paediatrica (1995); 84: 468-473.

15. Ezzo, G., & Ezzo, A. (1993). *Preparation for Parenting: Bringing God's Order to Your Baby's Day and Restful Sleep to Your Baby's Night* (4th ed.). Northridge, Calif.: Growing Families International Press.

16. Ezzo, G., & Bucknam, R. (2001). *On Becoming Babywise: Parenting Your Pre-toddler Five to Fifteen Months*. Simi Valley, CA: Parent-Wise Solutions.

17. Pearl, M., & Pearl, D. (20091994). *To Train Up a Child*. Pleasantville, Tenn.: NGJ Ministries.

18. Sears, Dr. William. SIDS: A Parent's Guide to Understanding and Preventing Sudden Infant Death Syndrome . Little Brown & Co, 1995. Print. **http://www.amazon.com/SIDS-Parents-Understanding-Preventing-Syndrome/dp/0316779121/ref=sr_1_1?s=books&ie=UTF8&qid=1360194660&sr=1-1&keywords=0316779121**

19. Feldman, R., Magori-Cohen, R., Galili, G., & Louzoun, Y. (2011, December 1). Mother and infant coordinate heart rhythms through episodes of interaction synchrony. Volume 34, Issue 4, December 2011, Pages 569–577, *Science Direct*. Retrieved April 15, 2014, from **http://www.sciencedirect.com/science/article/pii/S0163638311000749**

20. Onya Baby, . "Can babywearing eliminate the need for tummy time?." N.p., 04 02 2012. Web. Web. 15 Feb. 2013. **http://onyababy.com/blog/2012/02/can-babywearing-eliminate-the-need-for-tummy-time/**

21. Falco, Miriam. "New advice to prevent and correct flat head syndrome in babies." CNN Health. 28 Nov 2011: n. page. Web. 7 Feb. 2013. **http://thechart.blogs.cnn.com/2011/11/28/new-advice-to-prevent-and-correct-flat-head-syndrome-in-babies/**

22. GORD and Babywearing. (n.d.). *Reflux Infants Support Association*. Retrieved April 15, 2014, from **http://www.reflux.org.au/gord-and-babywearing/**

23. Medical Advisory Board, "IHDI Educational Statement." International Hip Dysplasia Institute. 2012: n. page. Web. 7 Feb. 2013.
http://www.hipdysplasia.org/Developmental-Dysplasia-Of-The-Hip/Prevention/Baby-Carriers-Seats-and-Other-Equipment/

24. Sacks, J. (2001, March 26). *Revelation: Torah From Heaven.*

25. *New Testament Greek Lexicon - New American Standard.* (n.d.). Retrieved March 20, 2014, from
http://www.biblestudytools.com/lexicons/greek/nas/

26. Sykes, J. B. (1976). *The Concise Oxford Dictionary of Current English: Based on the Oxford English Dictionary and its Supplements.* (6th ed.). Oxford, Eng.: Clarendon Press.

27. Ezzo, G., & Ezzo, A. M. (1990). *Growing Kids God's Way: For No Excuse Parenting* (3rd ed.). Northridge, Calif.: Growing Families International Press.

28. Dobson, J. C. (1992). *The New Dare to Discipline.* Wheaton, Ill.: Tyndale House Publishers.

29. Healy, Melissa. "The Mind Unchecked." Los Angeles Times 01 12 2009, Health n. pag. Web. 9 Oct. 2013.
http://latimesblogs.latimes.com/booster_shots/2009/12/the-mind-unchecked-is-babys-lack-of-selfcontrol-key-to-early-learning.html

30. Dobson, J. C. (1970). *Dare to Discipline.* Wheaton, Ill.: Tyndale House Publishers.

31. Ezzo, G., & Bucknam, R. (1994). *Babywise II: The Next Step.* Chatsworth, Calif.: Growing Families International.

32. Sandham, L. J., & Hicks, R. A. (1982, January 1). *.Forethought Development in Children.*
http://download.springer.com/static/pdf/26/art%253A10.3758%252FBF03330086.pdf?auth66=1397973703_f53aa98e905b80770ee68ef52a2dcc0f&ext=.pdf

33. Park, A. (2010, May 3). The Long-Term Effects of Spanking. *Time.* Retrieved March 25, 2014, from
http://content.time.com/time/magazine/article/0,9171,1983895,00.html

34. Canadian Medical Association Journal. (2012, February 6). Physical punishment of children potentially harmful to their long-term development. ScienceDaily. Retrieved April 17, 2014 from
www.sciencedaily.com/releases/2012/02/120206122447.htm

35. University of New Hampshire. (2009, September 25). Children Who Are Spanked Have Lower IQs, New Research Finds. ScienceDaily. Retrieved April 18, 2014 from
www.sciencedaily.com/releases/2009/09/090924231749.htm

36. M.D., W. S. (n.d.). Science Says: Excessive Crying Could Be Harmful. *Ask Dr Sears The Trusted Resource for Parents*. Retrieved March 20, 2014, from **http://www.askdrsears.com/topics/health-concerns/fussy-baby/science-says-excessive-crying-could-be-harmful**

37. Schore, M.D., A. N. (1996, January 1). Development and Psychopathology. *Cambridge Journals*. Retrieved April 15, 2014, from **http://journals.cambridge.org/action/displayAbstract;jsessionid=990094C5D998B7E9619347EE4256D369.journals?fromPage=online&aid=4495696**

38. *Roget's II: The New Thesaurus*. (1980). Boston: Houghton Mifflin.

39. Dobson, J. C. (2004). *The New Strong-Willed Child: Birth Through Adolescence*. Wheaton, Ill.: Tyndale House Publishers.

40. Latin Dictionary and Grammar Resources - Latdict. (n.d.). *Latin Dictionary and Grammar Resources - Latdict*. Retrieved March 20, 2014, from **http://www.latin-dictionary.net/**

41. Color Psychology. (n.d.). *The Meaning of Colors*. Retrieved April 15, 2014, from **https://resources.oncourse.iu.edu/access/content/user/rreagan/Filemanager_Public_Files/meaningofcolors.htm**

42. Esther, E. (2014). *Girl at the End of the World: My Escape from Fundamentalism in Search of Faith with a Future*. : Convergent Books .

The first three books in the Little Hearts Handbook series by L.R.Knost:

Two Thousand Kisses a Day: Gentle Parenting Through the Ages and Stages

Calm, Reassuring, Likable ~ Written in L.R.Knost's signature easy-to-read and conversational style, *Two Thousand Kisses a Day* offers an overview of gentle parenting from birth through young adulthood along with concrete suggestions and insights into how to implement gentle parenting in each stage of childhood. Her seasoned and practical approach based on extensive child development research and years of parent mentoring as well as over twenty-five years of parenting her six children is as likable as it is reassuring. Parents with children of any age will find this information-packed book with its bite-sized chapters and practical approach to parenting a helpful and encouraging addition to their home library, as well as a welcome gift for new or struggling parents.

Whispers Through Time: Communication Through the Ages and Stages of Childhood

Sweet, Funny, Insightful ~ Award-winning *Whispers Through Time* by L.R. Knost is destined to be a dog-eared favorite, passed down from generation to generation. L.R. Knost shows parents how to find their own answers for their own children and their own families in this guidebook that challenges conventional thinking with a wisdom born of experience and a healthy dose of research to back it up. Written with the same unique blend of sweetness and humor, grit and honesty, reassurance and insight that made L.R. Knost's first book, *Two Thousand Kisses a Day: Gentle Parenting Through the Ages and Stages*, a best-seller, *Whispers Through Time* has become a runaway hit in its own right.

Relaxed, Reassuring, Practical ~ Written by L.R.Knost, best-selling, award-winning author of *Two Thousand Kisses a Day* and *Whispers Through Time*, *The Gentle Parent: Positive, Practical, Effective Discipline* shares the simple secrets of a peaceful, happy home in the Three C's of gentle discipline–Connection, Communication, and Cooperation. In her signature relaxed and poetic style, L.R.Knost gently guides parents through the steps of applying the Three C's in real-life scenarios from tantrums to defiance to parenting a strong-willed child to healing a broken parent/child relationship. Practical and proven, this newest installment in the Little Hearts Handbook parenting series will be tucked into diaper bags, kept handy on nightstands, and shared with good friends for its research-backed, experience-based, and humor-rich insights, ideas, and inspiration.

Made in the USA
Monee, IL
12 September 2020

41913722R00134